THE 10 HOTTEST
CONSULTING PRACTICES

THE 10 HOTTEST CONSULTING PRACTICES

WHAT THEY ARE, HOW TO GET INTO THEM

Ron Tepper

JOHN WILEY & SONS, INC.

New York • Chichester • Brisbane • Toronto • Singapore

Library of Congress Cataloging-in-Publication Data:

Tepper, Ron, 1937–
    The 10 hottest consulting practices : What they are, how to get
into them / Ron Tepper.
        p.   cm.
    Includes index.
    ISBN 0-471-11000-0 (alk. paper)
    1. Consultants. I. Title.
HD69.C6T45   1995
001'.023'73—dc20   95-4261

Printed in the United States of America

10 9 8 7 6 5 4 3 2 1

Contents

THE 10 HOTTEST
CONSULTING PRACTICES

INTRODUCTION

"One person's misfortune can be another's opportunity." Nowhere is this axiom truer than in consulting, a profession that has become a bonanza of good fortune to numerous practitioners, thanks to the cutbacks that have riddled U.S. industry.

Downsizing has created giant voids in the traditional organization chart. Companies are lean and mean—and they need help. Many functions, from training and marketing to human resources, have been devastated by the cuts.

That's the bad news. Now for the good. Cutbacks have left companies seeking out consultants who could perform the functions of employees who were no longer around. While one segment of industry is suffering, another is booming. Many of those who were once working for corporations, now find themselves heading prosperous consulting firms.

Virtually every consulting field is in-demand. However, there are ten in particular, that are especially hot. These ten fields are not only booming today, but the demand for them is projected to increase even more as the year 2000 approaches.

Now, some more good news. Consulting is not what it used to be. In the 1980s, consultants were housed in plush, high-rise office buildings, they had lengthy lunches, long dinners, and played golf with clients on weekday afternoons. Expense was not an object.

1

There are still consulting firms operating out of downtown offices, however, a significant share of the consulting business is going to a new breed of practitioners who have spent less than $5,000 to open their doors, operate out of their homes, and generate six-figure incomes without hiring an employee.

The entrepreneurs running these ten different practices are aggressive, creative individuals, who are taking advantage of the 10 major changes that have hit consulting and U.S. industry in the 1990s; changes that are going to impact the consulting profession into the year 2000 and continue to make it—and these ten professions—the best entrepreneurial business opportunities in the country.

Although these ten consultants are in ten different fields, each has taken similar roads to the top. In *The 10 Hottest Consulting Professions: What They Are, How to Get into Them,* each consultant outlines the steps they took to not only start their enterprises, but build them. They also explain why their field is in-demand, and how potential entrepreneurs can find other areas with similar potential.

Some of these professionals have been in the field for more than a decade, while others opened their doors less than a year ago. In each case, they have built enormously successful practices, and are generating more income than they ever did while in the corporate world. They are a diverse group, and their backgrounds range from a former schoolteacher to an industrial engineer. Their fields are equally as diverse.

How these consultants picked their fields, developed clients, marketed their services, set fees, billed, and communicated with clients—all these steps and more—are laid out in a practical, how-to manner. By following their methods, any present, or potential, consultant can learn more about the industry, emulate their techniques, and have the same opportunity for success that this new breed in this newly revitalized industry are enjoying.

The ten hottest consulting professions are:

• *Strategic Alliance/Strategic Development.* For several years, companies have been concentrating on cutting costs. Now, they want to expand and develop sales for both new and old product lines. The Strategic Alliance/Strategic Development consultant provides the expertise that enables companies to not only serve their present clients more professionally (and generate additional sales), but they also help evaluate where firms can go to broaden their market.

Jack Branberg is a marketing consultant, who carefully examines a company and its present position. He is an idea man, who knows sales and distribution. Branberg is sought after by companies throughout the world because of his expertise. He is analytical; a perfectionist. Before opening his own practice, he was a partner in Peat Marwick, and head of Ross Perot's EDS West Coast consulting division. He is one of the few consultants who operates out of an office that is not his home—but for a good reason.

- *Communications/PR (Public Relations).* With the chaos created internally by downsizing, and the diminishing impact of advertising on external customers, this field has suddenly emerged as critically important. Adding to the demand for Communications/PR practitioners, is the increasing scrutiny that companies are encountering from the media. Communications/PR and "crisis" professionals such as Carol Beekman, are typical of the new breed of fast-paced consultants who are entering this field. Beekman paid her dues by spending more than a decade in the private sector, where she learned her profession. Her agency background has given her special expertise in being able to handle clients. The proof of her ability is in the fact her company was in the black within 30 days after she opened.

- *Executive Search Consultant.* These professionals are more commonly known as "headhunters." With the enormous cutbacks, companies have downsized their human resource (HR) departments, yet they still need top-flight skilled professionals. Increasingly, they are turning to executive search consultants, who are not only saving them time, but money. An executive search consultant can find the candidate, and usually spend less money doing it. The newest twist to the executive search field, however, is the hottest—a specialized, menu-based practice where companies can pick and choose the executive search services they need.

Dan Potter has perfected the menu-based, specialized approach. Potter is an innovative, ambitious former A.T. Kearney consultant, who developed this technique. As of this writing, he was the only headhunting practitioner who specialized in health care and utilized the menu-based system. The innovative technique enabled him to open his home office without a client, and in just over a year his income was in the six-figure range.

• *Site Services/Meeting Planning.* Often overlooked but growing rapidly. With "compact," rightsized organizations becoming the norm, meetings have become more important—and so have meeting planners. Companies do not have the resources to devote to this function, and they are reaching outside more than ever. The profession is growing at a pace second to none.

Laurie Mirman, a hard-working, bright entrepreneur, has been at the forefront of this growth with her site services/meeting planning business. Her story is the type on which the American Dream is built. Ten years ago, she opened her own practice because no one would give her a job. Today, she has ten employees (she is one of the few consultants who hires full-timers) and is doubling her office size. Her business is one that will generate a comfortable six-figure income this year.

• *Sales Training Consultant.* The heart of any enterprise is sales, and next to the actual "order," the most critical aspect is making sure that every salesperson is productive and efficient. Many companies have abandoned in-house sales training, using outside resources instead. Top sales trainers, such as Cindy Novotny, have built enormous practices during the past few years. With international markets opening, this field has only one way to go—up.

Novotny's story is similar to Mirman's. A success story that shows what hard work and determination can do. Novotny gave up a successful corporate life to start her own sales training firm. Without clients or funds, she opened what has become one of the most successful international sales training firms in the country. Novotny is highly disciplined, and her daily routine is structured, a factor that has enabled her to go from no clients to a full house. Like many consultants, she operates out of her home and does not have any employees.

• *Sales and Marketing Consultant.* How do you take your products and services to market? Where are the opportunities? Sales, once again, is the heartbeat of the corporation, and sales and marketing consultants are being called on increasingly to assist internal departments in finding opportunities and evaluating new products and services before they are put into the field. (Notice the difference between this profession and Strategic Alliance/Strategic Development. Consultants in this area work extensively with new products).

Brad Leggett, who has built one of the most successful practices in the country, is relatively new to the business. He opened his doors a few years ago, but had an excellent background, consisting of more than 15 years in the high-tech field. Since that time, this innovative practitioner has built an incredibly successful practice in two industries—one of the few consultants able to make that claim. Leggett goes it alone, too, but thanks to a network of associates, he can compete head-to-head with any major consulting organization.

- *Management Consultant.* This is a new twist to an old field. The demand from customers for improved, reliable products and services has thrust the management consultant into a growing niche. How can a company improve its production? Build relationships with its customers? Lay out factories and plants so that they are more efficient and quality oriented?

Management consultant Mike Green provides those answers. Casual and laid back best describes this West Coast entrepreneur, who started his practice six years ago. Green, who operates a practice without employees, does many things differently, and can handle some of the biggest projects in the country thanks to the relationships he has built with other consultants around the country. Green also has a unique business-building approach, and utilizes direct mail in a manner that few have thought about.

- *Outplacement.* The growing number of blue and white collar workers losing their jobs, and the increasing pressure of employee lawsuits, has opened an entire new area of opportunity for outplacement practitioners. Rudy Dew is the epitome of success in this field. From a small, one office beginning, Dew has become an international outplacement consultant with offices in Tokyo as well as the rest of the United States. Dew's area, which many thought to be slowing, is growing rapidly thanks to his marketing expertise, and his ability to target outplacement services to companies that are dealing with both blue and white collar workers.

- *Compensation.* The environment in the workplace has changed, and employees expect methods of determining compensation to change, too. Companies are abandoning the typical merit increases, revising bonus plans, and searching for new and innovative ways to reward productive employees. Pressure to introduce these new plans grows daily, as employees increasingly question management and the decisions that are being made.

Andrea Needham is an innovator who is on the cutting edge of this profession, which is one of the fastest growing in the country. Every company is reevaluating the traditional way of paying workers, and Needham's sought after advice, which goes back nearly 20 years, has transformed her practice into one of the hottest in the country.

- *Reorganization/Organization.* The old pyramid-style organization chart is obsolete. Companies are searching for new, more efficient approaches. Gerry Stern launched his company nine years ago, and developed one of the most clever marketing tools in the industry—the *Stern SourceFinder*. An innovator, Stern also developed the "virtual corporation," a concept that brings together a team of top consultants to work on a project and split the profits. The virtual corporation has application in every consulting field and has enabled Stern to compete successfully with the biggest consulting firms in the country.

CHAPTER 1

CONSULTING—WHERE IT IS, WHERE IT IS GOING, AND WHY THESE 10 FIELDS ARE HOT

Few industries have changed more in such a short span of time than consulting. And few professions are producing as much opportunity. For the 1990s and into the year 2000, there is no better enterprise for an entrepreneur to enter.

In the past decade, there has been a revolution in the industry. Clients have changed, their demands are different, profits are at an all-time high, overhead is at an all-time low, and the need for practitioners is growing daily.

Imagine a business in which it does not matter where your office is located. You can work out of your home, without the location negatively impacting your practice.

Imagine a business into which you do not have to pour capital for hiring additional consultants in order to expand the enterprise. You can hire the best skilled professionals in the market, and on a part-time or contract basis.

Imagine a business where you can compete—on equal terms—against rival companies 10 and 20 times your size; against major consulting companies that have resources that dwarf those of your enterprise.

NO ADVERTISING NEEDED

Imagine a business where relationships count more than all the advertising in the world; where clients hire you on the basis of your capabilities and past performance.

This is a picture of consulting in the final half-decade of the twentieth century. This is why one of the most promising industries—for the entrepreneur—in America is consulting.

In a recent *Business Week* cover story ("The Craze for Consultants"), the magazine points out that in 1993, AT&T spent an astounding $347 million on consulting and research services—a figure nearly triple the company's expenditure in 1990.

While the demand for tax and auditing services of most Big 6 accounting firms remained flat during the first half of 1994, the demand for consultants from those companies grew almost 10 percent. Douglas Jacobs, managing partner with Arthur Andersen & Co.'s Irvine (CA) office said "whether we are coming out of a recession or not, our core business will continue to be flat. Clients are demanding more value-added services, such as consulting."

Chris Massey, managing partner, Deloitte & Touche, says their consulting business jumped from 15 percent of their total billing in 1993, to 25 percent in 1994. And, the number of consultants on staff jumped 9 percent.

Eighty thousand consultants—from small one- and two-person shops to global conglomerates—generated $17 billion in 1993 for the advice they gave. That figure was 10 percent higher than the previous year, with expenditures for the remainder of the decade forecast to be just as growth-oriented.

THE 10 HOTTEST FIELDS

Included in those figures is the revenue generated by the ten consultants featured in this book. They are phenomenally successful, and run the gamut from management and strategic practitioners to communications and training consultants. Each has carved a special niche, and seven out of the ten have built thriving practices without hiring any employees.

Most have been in business less than a decade, and some entered the field when consulting was thought to be a mature industry on the wane—an industry that had seen its better days.

What's happened? What elements took a relatively slow growing, mundane business and turned it into one of the success stories of the 1990s? And, why are these ten consulting fields so hot?

Major Changes

Changes in operating have impacted every consultant. The ten major ones are:

1. *Project versus Retainer.* Consultants used to depend on retainers, and seldom would they take a job unless the client was willing to put them on one. In the past few years, that has changed. Projects have become the norm in the business. Seldom will a client give a consultant a retainer—money is too tight.

Projects enable consultants to concentrate on one specific area, for a limited time. They are also a way for consultants to display their expertise to clients, and the client has an easier time measuring the project's progress. If a consultant does a good job, the project may lead to a retainer or another project.

2. *Relationship Marketing.* This has become one of the most important growth areas in the field. Instead of networking—a process where consultants used to hand out business cards at Chamber of Commerce mixers—consultants are concentrating on building relationships. That is, they get to know other consultants and business-

people. Through relationship marketing, consultants have been able to generate clients, referrals, and, most important, assistance from other talented professionals when they get a project that requires additional help.

In the past, consultants had a difficult time competing with major consulting firms when it came to vying for larger clients. That is no longer the case. Thanks to relationship marketing, one-person consulting shops can compete head-on with large, Big 6 firms—and come out on top. Relationship marketing has enabled the one-person shop to bring in skilled, part-time professionals to help "pitch" clients and work on the account. The ability to get professionals on a part-time or project basis, has even given some consultants a distinct advantage over the large consulting enterprises.

3. *Home Office.* The expensive suite in a high-rise building is out; the home office is in. Clients know that consultants work out of their homes, and it *does not* make a difference. The home office is viewed as a low overhead feature that translates to savings for clients on fees and expenses.

4. *Implementation.* In the past, consultants used to interview the client and their employees, determine the problem, develop a solution, and hand in a plan. Many times, the plan never made it off the shelf. The problem the consultant had been called in to solve remained—because there was no one to guide the implementation. Now, clients want consultants involved in the implementation phase. Thus, the client gets to see the results, and if the consultant has come up with an innovative solution, it not only turns into a positive relationship with the client, but more often than not it will lead to additional business. Implementation has strengthened the relationship between client and consultant.

5. *No Employees.* Consultants are able to operate without hiring full-time assistants and/or other consultants. This has enabled the practitioner to create and run a firm with extremely low overhead; overhead so low that the one-person shop can compete head-on with major consulting firms, and offer more service for less money.

6. *Agency Factor.* A growing number of consultants have consulting agency background, a factor that has made them more proficient

in their profession. Agencies not only train consultants how to sell clients on services, but how to deal with them as well.

7. *Part-Time Consultants.* In the past, one- or two-person consulting practices found themselves competing with part-timers as well as large consulting companies. Now, with the restructuring of U.S. industry, prospective clients are no longer enamoured with part-timers. They want full-time professionals. By opping for the full-timer, prospective clients have removed one of the players in the industry, and created more demand for the full-time practitioner.

8. *Female Consultants.* One of the most noteworthy developments in the past few years, was that many large corporations began hiring women. This enabled numerous women to get excellent management experience at the corporate level and work with external consultants at the same time. It provided the opportunity for the growing number of female consultants who are opening their own practices.

9. *The Downsized Corporation.* The impact of downsizing is greater than anyone imagined. Entire human resource (HR) and training departments have been disbanded. Marketing staffs have been cutback; employees no longer have undying loyalty to the corporation; and with international marketing emerging, companies have run into new demands, ranging from sales to compensation—and they do not have the staff to answer those demands.

10. *Experience.* Do what you know . . . and you better know it. In the past, nearly anyone who was in business could claim the consulting tag. They could get by with minimal industry experience, because not many clients really knew what consultants should be doing, and what the results should be. That is no longer the case. Clients want consultants who know their fields, because they not only have to solve problems, but the contemporary consultant also has to implement those solutions. Additionally, many of today's clients were once consultants themselves, and they have the ability to objectively—and accurately—evaluate the practitioner's expertise. Thus, experience and knowledge have taken on a new emphasis.

Now, a closer look at some of those changes and how they have impacted the consulting industry. Credit the explosion of such concepts as Total Quality Management (TQM), ISO 9000, reengineering, downsizing, rightsizing, restructuring, globalization, relationship marketing, and so on.

There are few companies that illustrate a better example of why the demand for consultants is growing than Union Carbide. A few years ago, the company went through a companywide restructuring, designed to cut $400 million in costs.

The Chief Financial Officer (CFO) decided to check on the firm's financial operations to see how well it was doing when compared to the accounting departments of other major corporations. To his dismay, he found that in some areas—such as journal entries—Union Carbide was spending ten times more than other firms their size. That was all it took. The company cut 200 positions and saved $20 million in salaries.

Union Carbide found what other large conglomerates had run into. They spent so much time paring back, cutting costs, and slimming down, the number crunchers—accountants—or the people who did the counting kept multiplying. Just as companies had gone through a day of reckoning for marketing, training, and sales, there was now a day of reckoning for accountants.

OUTSOURCING

Companies have found that in most cases, cutting back full-time personnel saves enough money to hire a part-time consultant, get the job done, and have cash left over.

Although the wholesale downsizing has slowed, the lean, mean mentality—in all departments—has not. Companies are not hiring. They are outsourcing wherever possible. And the recipient of the outsourced business is usually a consultant.

Recent college graduates have found this to be painfully true. The hiring of new college graduates in the 1993–1994 academic year was up only 2.2 percent over the previous year. And, that figure follows four years of decline. Now, the shocker—one-fifth of those graduates were hired for temporary or contractual positions, much as a firm would hire a consultant.

Even giants such as General Motors have gone heavily into the search for consultants versus full-time employees. General Motors recently hired A.T. Kearney, a large Chicago-based consulting firm, for advice in streamlining and speeding the process of creating new models. Normally, this would have been an internal project. Now, it is in the hands of a consulting firm.

All these cutbacks have created another scenario. Corporate Managers are being burned out. Most of those that are not on fire, have lost their enthusiasm because they are constantly on deadlines, facing pressures, and stuck with the reality that there is not enough time to get everything done—because there are not enough people.

In a recent survey in *USA Today,* nearly two-thirds of those workers/managers who responded said they "are always or frequently rushed." Of these, 26 percent have not taken a vacation in the past 12 months. Almost half the workers surveyed by Families and Work Institute say job demands are excessive rather than manageable. One-third seriously think about quitting because of job stress.

An Arthur D. Little survey of 350 companies that have downsized shows only 17 percent satisfied with the results. Savings that were promised have not materialized because of low morale from over-worked employees.

OPPORTUNITIES FOR ONE-PERSON FIRMS

What does this have to do with consulting? A growing number of companies are trying to turn the situation around. Some are actually forcing employees to take vacation. While others are trying to ease the load by bringing in more people to handle projects, more consultants.

All these elements spurred consulting's growth and have presented opportunities to small, entrepreneurial one-person consulting practices. At the same time, the major consulting firms (McKinsey & Company, Coopers & Lybrand, Monitor, Ernst & Young) have been swamped with business. In fact, it is not uncommon to find some of the large firms with total contracts for more than $100 million.

The business has changed—radically. Take, for instance, the case of Joseph H. Morgan. Morgan was a prosperous sales training consultant who had built an enormously successful practice. He operated out of a palatial, high-rise office building in southern California, catering to some of the most elite Fortune 500 companies in the country.

It was not unusual to find him at lengthy, expensive lunches with clientele who were CEOs of some of the best-known, publicly held companies in the United States. His Friday afternoon ritual almost always included an early departure from his office, capped by an afternoon at the golf course with several clients.

His country club dues were equivalent to what many of his peers grossed during a six-month period. When the greying, distinguished businessman traveled, it was always first class. Most of his business, however, was local, where there were many companies, all anxious to hire Morgan.

He was the epitome of success. He belonged to the local Rotary, was chairman of the YMCA membership committee, served as a director on a non-profit corporation, and was frequently mentioned as a possible mayoral or council candidate.

Morgan had built one of the largest consulting practices in the western half of the country. His staff consisted of more than two dozen trainers, four secretaries, a fully-staffed mailroom, data processing operator, and a full-time accountant.

His billings topped $6 million a year, with nearly 40 percent going to overhead. His monthly entertainment tab often topped $5,000.

Typically, a client would call him in for a study. Morgan would peruse the company, interview executives, determine the problem, come back with a proposal that was usually accepted, work out the solutions, hand it to management—and leave. Along the way, he might alienate or frighten the staff of a department or two within the company.

Morgan's heyday was a decade before the previously mentioned story was published in *Business Week*. He flourished in an era—the mid-1980s—when consultants were hired more for their office decor and connections than for their knowledge.

Today, companies in search of consulting expertise, do not have the time to send a manager out to be wined and dined by a practitioner. Nor, do they have the time to visit the consultant's office.

They want the practitioner to come to them. They want to hire the right person for the project the first time around and they want the problem not only identified, but solved. The focus has changed.

Andrea Needham, a compensation consultant, and one of the ten top practitioners in this book, explains the Morgan phenomena of the 1980s. "In the 1980s, our industry was dominated by MBAs and academic people. They were technically oriented and felt they had an answer for everything. That was not true, because there was not an answer for every situation. But, there were not many consultants around who would admit they did not know. It hurt the business and their credibility."

Today, the Joseph Morgan-style operation is gone—a dinosaur. It has been replaced by aggressive, young consultants such as Needham, who approach clients and problems differently. Needham and others no longer come in, research, interview, analyze, prepare a report, deliver it, and leave.

Today, consultants want to be part of the solution. They form teams with management and employees and work together to solve problems. Instead of submitting reports and leaving, successful consultants help implement them.

COMPENSATION CONSULTANTS ON RISE

"This is one of the most exciting times to be in this business," says Needham. She knows. Needham is in a field that is going through enormous changes: compensation. How do you pay people? What kind of incentives do you give them? Why should senior managers get greater bonuses than the hourly worker, when the quality and output of the product/service is dependent just as much on the hourly as the manager?

Since downsizing started, companies have run into these problems even more. Moral and loyalty have become a major problem. Compensation is one way to deal with the problem, however, it has to be handled correctly. Needham is one of the few who knows how to analyze a company, find the problems, talk to the workers, and devise a plan that gets the firm working as a whole.

"Our job is to be visionaries. Not to do for the client, but to teach the client how to do. To help them develop strategies and practical, how to solutions for the future."

GROWTH OF HOME OFFICE

Practical is a word that is sweeping the industry. Instead of the expensive office suites of the Morgan era, practitioners work out of their home. A decade ago, a home office would have been the kiss of death. Prospects would have looked upon consultants as part-timers, unprofessional. Today, clients know and accept home offices as a way of making consulting more affordable to them.

Part of the acceptance is due to technology. Clients know that capable consultants can operate out of anywhere and communicate instantly thanks to fax, modems, computers, and cellular telephones. They also understand that the more reasonable the rent/overhead, the lower the fee.

DEMAND FOR SALES TRAINING CONSULTANTS

Cindy Novotny, another top consultant, works out of her Orange County (CA) home and has fax, modem, computer, laser printer, and telephone. She does not play golf, her overhead is minimal, and her start-up costs were under $5,000.

But, Novotny offers one of the most critical services required by companies—sales training. Regardless of how lean and mean a corporation is, without a good, capable sales force it is going nowhere. Unfortunately for most companies, but fortunately for Novotny, training is one of those functions that was eliminated in the first or second downsizing wave. It is almost always outsourced, and as more capable training consultants appear, there are more firms that believe they can eliminate their internal staff.

Novotny is in such demand that she travels more than 300 days a year to companies requiring her services. If she wanted, she could be on the road at another company training site, every day. Although the health of individual industries is difficult to project, one thing can be said with relative certainty—companies need salespeople, and salespeople will always need good training.

Novotny does not have employees, nor does she want any. She works on a project basis, rather than retainer, and can tap resources for assistance whenever she wants it, thanks to the many relationships she has built with other sales trainers.

GROWTH OF RELATIONSHIP MARKETING

Novotny views other sales trainers as allies, not competitors. She frequently hires one or two to help her when a project demands it. Novotny, however, did not find assistance through networking. The term has fallen out of favor, especially among consultants. Today, Novotny and other practitioners develop contacts and clients through "relationship marketing."

Networking was typified by Chamber of Commerce mixers, and people trading business cards. Trying to get leads and a marketing edge from someone. If one person referred someone to the other the favor would be returned. Most of the time, the consultant knew little about the person with whom they networked. Each had one thing in common—they were looking for business.

Contemporary consultants shy away from networking, and practice relationship marketing. Relationship marketing means getting to know someone and their abilities before you recommend them. Relationship marketing does not mean a casual, one-time encounter and exchange of business cards. It refers to feeling confident about the person you recommend, because you have built a relationship with them and know what they can do.

Brad Leggett, another top ten consultant, explains relationship marketing. "The initial component is high visibility. In other words, if you are in the consulting field, you make sure others see you. Step two is you look around and say what can I do for other people? None of those things initially mean business, but they enable you to build relationships. You open the doors and keep them open. Build the right relationships, and sooner or later the business will come."

DEMAND FOR SALES/MARKETING ON UPSWING

Business has come to Leggett in droves. He deals in an area that can be extremely frustrating for firms—sales and marketing. Today, companies are being barraged by sales and marketing problems. Everything from global marketing problems to selling high priced, high quality domestic goods.

How can a producer of widget X compete? Where should they target their efforts? Should they? Should they concentrate on one industry? How can they get better distribution? Should they even release the product and/or service?

Leggett provides the answers, and his services are in demand. Last year, more than 95 percent of all new products and services that were introduced flopped. Billions of dollars were spent on them. Yet, new products are the lifeblood of industry. Regardless of the economy, companies must continue to produce new products, because the U.S. market is one of change. What was good yesterday, may no longer be bought tomorrow. Leggett helps companies determine what will be purchased and by whom. He also helps them find the right distribution channel for their goods.

CONSULTING SPECIALIZATION

Leggett can save a company millions, perhaps more. He has made his services even more valuable by specializing in industrial goods. By doing so, he has quickly become known in the industry as the consultant to talk to when it comes time to develop a strategy for a new industrial product.

"Companies," explains the sales/marketing consultant, "are in dire need of sales strategies. They may have a great product, and they may know where they want to go, but how do they get there? That's what they are calling about. In the old days, they had a staff of sales and marketing people ready to answer those questions. Not any more."

Carol Beekman (communications/PR) develops strategies, too. Her firm was profitable from day one and for good reason. Beekman is in a field that has been drastically impacted by downsizing. Companies have always looked on communications as an area that can be cutback. And, in the late 1980s, they cut it drastically.

Then, a funny thing happened. Managers found they had to communicate effectively to the employees who remained. One problem, there was no one left in the communication department to write and produce the communication vehicles. There was no one around to keep employees informed, or to handle crisis situations, such as an accident in the plant; a product that was found to have a defect.

Enter Beekman. Having a talent for written communication, she can help a company keep its employees informed as well as happy. Communication in today's environment is critical. Companies do not want to lose employees, and Beekman offers a way to help keep them.

"In the past, companies rarely looked upon communications and public relations as being important. They were viewed as implementation functions, rather than a part of the firm's strategic direction. Today, companies realize that communications and public relations can be critically important when it comes to determining where you are going and how you are going to get there."

A second driver is the realization on the part of many firms that advertising is not a cure-all. Media has become more fragmented—from commercial television to talk radio and cable television. Who is watching what? How can the dollars possibly cover all these outlets? They cannot. Customers and consumers have grown more sophisticated. They recognize advertising, and know the company has paid for it. But, public relations is more subtle. It carries enormous credibility, and that is something every firm wants today.

"Just imagine what a positive newspaper article can mean to a firm when its customers see it," says Beekman. "It does not carry any of the connotations that an ad may have. The customer does not know a communications/public relations specialist sold the media on doing that positive story. With advertising, they know the space was bought."

Public relations has also caught the eye of management because it is a relatively inexpensive tool. It costs a fraction of what advertising costs. With smaller budgets, and more closely watched bottom lines, the communications/public relations area has taken on a new importance.

Companies look at public relations not only as an adjunct to advertising, but in many cases some firms are using it as their prime marketing thrust. This is especially true in the entertainment industry, where word-of-mouth and the endorsement of a critic in print, means much more to a motion picture or play than advertising.

In business, there has been a growing need for competent public relations/communications counselors for another reason—the growing adversarial nature of the media toward industry.

Many writers and television reporters interview CEOs and examine companies with their sole motivation being to find something wrong with the enterprise. In other cases, firms find themselves in a "crisis" situation. That is, there has been an accident, spoilage in a product, or something else that has led to illness or injury.

In these situations, competent public relations/communications counseling can mean the survival of a company. Take, for instance, the handling of Tylenol.

Some years ago, someone tampered with the product, inserted poison, and contaminated Tylenol was found in several retail establishments. When one person died, panic ensued and sales of the product dropped to zero almost overnight. Analysts within the industry predicted that because of the tragedy, the name—and the product—would never be able to be marketed again.

Tylenol acted quickly and decisively. With clear, concise advice from its communication department, the company announced that it was immediately withdrawing all product from the market, and new "tamper proof" bottles would be substituted.

The fast action addressed the concerns of the consumer, and enabled the company to make a phenomenal comeback with the product. Today, Tylenol enjoys a healthy market share thanks to a clear-cut communication's policy.

The value of rapid communications has not escaped other companies, especially those that are prone to run into controversial issues, such as Tylenol. The demands from these companies, as well as other firms that see the need for clear communications, have enabled Beekman and other PR/communications consultants to open their doors without ever going through a day of red ink.

NEW CONSULTING NICHE

Another area that has seen an upswing in demand is headhunting—or executive search. It is ironic in an era when downsizing has displaced so many executives, that there is a need for an executive search firm, but there is. Top executive search consultants have always been sought out, and now one of the top headhunters in the country, Dan Potter, has taken executive search to a new level and created one of the hottest consulting fields in the industry.

Potter specializes in executive search, but he does more than the norm. He has put two new twists to an old profession: First, he specializes (health care) and second, he has developed a "menu of executive search services" that a company can pick from.

Potter came along at a time when companies needed executive search firms. The human resource departments were understaffed and did not have the time or personnel to search for executives. Additionally, Potter's approach gave them a way to escape the normal, heavy advertising expenditure it took to find an executive.

Typical headhunters charge up to 30 percent of an executive's annual salary (and bonus) to find a candidate. With that kind of incentive, headhunters sometimes recommend marginal candidates, in an effort to earn their fee.

Potter knew the process and saw an opportunity. Instead of charging a percentage, Potter asks a flat fee, and, at the same time, he offers the client a "menu of services," everything from developing a list of candidates to helping at the interview stage. The client picks and chooses. Regardless of how much of the menu they select, Potter's fees are still lower than those of his competitors. The menu-driven headhunter has become one of the busiest in the industry.

OUTPLACEMENT CONSULTING ON RISE

Rudy Dew is busy, too. In a way, his business is similar to Potter's. However, instead of trying to find job candidates, he looks for jobs for his candidates. Rudy runs a sophisticated, technologically oriented outplacement firm. That's where he has jumped ahead of the competition.

Dew's approach is partially computer-driven. Every executive who comes to him for help, ends up operating a computer and searching through data that will give them information on companies—who runs them, what they need, and so on—throughout the United States.

Dew's computerized approach has given him an edge, but American industry has done its share, too. With the abundance of laws that have been passed to protect workers, companies are concerned about possible lawsuits when they have to layoff or cutback. Dew offers an alternative to the problem. His firm does everything from counsel the company and its executives, to developing a program and helping the executive find a job.

Using this service is cost-effective for clients, and can save an enterprise thousands—sometimes millions—in legal fees. Unfortunately (but fortunately for Dew), the layoff rate for U.S. companies has slowed, but it is still going on—and Dew's services are in-demand more than ever.

REORGANIZATION CONSULTING EMERGES

The change in U.S. industry has impacted Gerry Stern's business as well. Stern specializes in "reorganization"—helping companies find a new way to do old things. Stern reshuffles organization charts and structures them so that employees can work more effectively and efficiently.

The driving force behind the demand for Stern's services is the changing face of U.S. industry. In the past, organizations had pyramid-shaped charts, with the box at the top usually belonging to the president.

Now, there are more boxes than employees. Companies cannot function as they did before. Yet, companies need to be more productive than ever. That's where Stern comes in. He delves into corporations and redesigns the organization.

When you cut numbers in a company, problems emerge. Employees are unhappy. A 10 percent cut in manufacturing personnel may impact a company and the attitude of its workers much more than a 10 percent cut in accounting.

The way companies are organized may need to change. "In many companies, despite being grateful that they have jobs, employees are unhappy because they feel they may have too great a share of the workload, and too little a piece of the pie. Companies are coming to the realization that reorganization is more complex than just eliminating a couple of boxes on the organization chart."

Stern brings an expertise to the market that every company needs. How can they reshuffle remaining employees to get the most out of their efforts? And, at the same time, satisfy a worker who may have lost faith in the organization. It is a challenge that almost every company in America faces. A challenge that has opened an enormous avenue of opportunity for consultants.

NEW MANAGEMENT CONSULTING THRUST

Mike Green has found opportunity, too. The former engineer is busy because he is one of the recognized management consulting pros when it comes to everything from quality control to moving a factory.

Business is constantly moving; some companies grow and need more space, while others need less. Some companies need to monitor their quality, while others are interested in new quality initiatives like "ISO 9000." Green knows it all. Especially ISO 9000, a European service and product quality measurement system that enables companies to improve their quality.

ISO 9000 is becoming critically important to many manufacturers, because a growing number of companies will not buy their products unless they have gone through ISO 9000 and been certified. Green can help. He knows it, and that's one reason his area has become one of the hottest to emerge in recent years.

THE STRATEGIC ALLIANCE CONSULTANT

Jack Branberg is in another area that has seen increasing demand from clients. Branberg is called a "strategic development" or "strategic alliance" consultant. For years, clients were trying to cut expenses, and they came to consultants to help them. Now, they realize they have cut as much as possible, and the only way to increase revenue is to generate more revenue. Strategic development consultants such as Branberg do exactly that.

He focuses on how to improve their revenue flow; he looks at the industry; does an internal assessment of the company's ability to deliver products; he examines ways in which manufacturers, service companies, and others can better (and more profitably) serve their customers. He also looks at potential new customers for products, and how his client can reach them.

In simple terms, Branberg increases sales. He may do it through new alliances for the client, or by improving old ones. He is a sales, marketing, and distribution manager rolled up into one. And those skills are among the most valuable in industry today.

MEETING/CONVENTION CONSULTANTS FILL VOID

Laurie Mirman offers a service that is growing in value, too. She's a meeting planner, a consulting service which has taken off in the past four years. Meeting planners used to occupy offices within corporations, however, with the reshuffling of industry, many companies have dropped their meeting planning departments.

Still, every corporation needs to hold meetings—they have to bring sales people, distributors, agents, employees, and others together at some time to plan and kick-off new products and services. But, they do not have the time (or resources) to have someone plan the meeting, book the hotel, and schedule the dates.

Enter Mirman's company. She not only does that, but she saves a firm money. Mirman has negotiated with virtually every hotel chain in the country, and not only books the rooms and schedules the meetings, but she saves a company thousands, sometimes tens of thousands of dollars, with her expertise and negotiated rates.

RELATIONSHIP MARKETING KEY TO GROWTH

Answering needs and providing special, innovative services have made each of these consulting professions the hottest in the country.

And their principals have become some of the most profitable entre-preneurs as well. Much of the credit for the growth and profitability of these firms goes to the technique called relationship marketing.

Relationship marketing has enabled consultants to grow their businesses without hiring permanent employees. Branberg works with a "consortium" of former Chief Operating Officers (CEOs). He can call any—or all—to help him with a project, and they are com-pensated on the basis of the one job. He has a "relationship" with them.

Novotny has a similar arrangement, as does Needham. Carol Beekman has built relationships with a number of associates who all have their own businesses, but each is connected to the public re-lations/communications area in some way. One, for example, has a design firm, another an advertising agency, and a third is a free-lance writer.

"I can farm out work anytime," she says, "and feel comfortable. However, if I had not taken the time to get to know these people, I would probably feel uneasy. Building the relationships has given me confidence in their ability. I know they will deliver, and there is no need for me to hire full-time copywriters and designers."

Relationship marketing means building rapport and trust with clients, as well as your peers, competitors, and those who can recom-mend business. It may sound odd building a bridge with a competi-tor, however, on numerous occasions one consultant will recommend another. This usually happens if the practitioner who provides the recommendation is either too loaded down with clients, or the prospect asks for something they cannot handle.

Branberg says relationship marketing is one of the key, critical changes in the profession. "Consulting has become relationship-oriented. People have to trust you before they recommend your services, or before they hire you. It is definitely a change for the better."

Dew says relationship marketing has become the one ingredient that every consultant needs to master in order to be successful. "It has made consultants realize that they have to partner with clients."

Relationship marketing has enabled consulting firms to grow with-out hiring; to increase billing without upping overhead. Green says every industry is doing the same thing. "No one is hiring permanent employees if they can avoid it. If you build a solid relationship, a consultant can retain a peer for a project with confidence they will do the job."

Although numerous consulting firms have shied away from hiring staff, the technique does not work in every industry. Mirman's meeting planning firm is one.

"Our business is labor intensive, and it takes full-time follow-up. This year we will handle more than 600 meetings, and it would be impossible for me to find—and keep tabs on—enough freelancers. Hiring part-timers in meeting planning would be inefficient. Remember, they have to do follow-up after the project is completed."

HOW SKILL LEVELS IMPACT GROWTH

Regardless of whether a consultant uses freelancers or hires internally, relationships are critical. Consultants have learned it is a mistake to hire someone without knowing their skill level. Clients are aware of the importance of knowing a consultant and their skill levels before hiring, too. A decade ago, a major corporation could spend the funds, hire a consultant, realize their mistake, and hire someone else. They had the capital; today, they do not. Abilities are scrutinized before a commitment is made by clients or consultants.

Branberg tells of a client for whom he handled several projects. During the years they worked together, the relationship developed into a solid bond. The client was confident of Branberg's ability.

"One day, the client called. He was moving offices and he asked if I would recommend an office furniture company. I don't know anything about office furniture, but it shows how powerful relationship marketing can be. If we had not built a solid relationship, the client would never have called to ask that question. It showed that he had faith in my judgment."

Relationship marketing has ushered in other changes. In the Morgan era, consultants tried to sell clients on everything from retainers to year-long (or more) contracts. Even before they found out what the client needed, there was a pitch for an ongoing retainer. The prime discussion usually centered around the benefit the client would receive by having a consultant on retainer; ready to solve any problem.

Disappearance of Retainers

"Today," says Branberg, "successful consultants are not after retainers or long-term commitments. Often we are hired for one specific project and nothing beyond."

Consultants have to become accustomed to this approach. Companies cannot—or will not—afford retainers. Most clients want one project at a time. The faster the consultant recognizes this desire—and gears his or her services to handle projects—the faster success will come.

As the project gets underway, other issues and problems surface. These issues may lead to additional projects. If the project contracted for is successfully managed, the client will want to partner with you again. As Branberg says, "Build the relationship; be a partner. If you do, business will take care of itself."

Relationship marketing has also made it possible for solo practitioners to compete with large, consulting conglomerates, such as Peat, Marwick and McKinsey. In the past, consulting companies had to staff up in order to go head-to-head with their large competitors. Not any more. Small, entrepreneurial companies are building relationships with former CEOs, other consultants, and skilled professional managers, who may have lost their positions during a downsizing.

When these consulting firms approach a prospect and see the need, they take along one, two, or more of these professionals. It's impressive to walk into the office of a prospective client with a former CEO or senior vice president. It has given the one-person shop additional muscle.

VIRTUAL CORPORATION: CREATIVE WAY TO PARTNER

Stern has been in business for years, but always had a difficult time when he vied for business against large consulting firms. Industry has come around, and today thanks to the relationships he has built, Stern can enter a prospective client's office with heavyweight, talented consulting associates who are ready to assist him on any project. None are employees.

Stern has developed what he calls a "virtual corporation." The corporation is temporary, and consists of an array of talented consultants, all with different skills. Stern brings them together for large projects, where they construct a joint proposal, and if the project is won, all those in the corporation sign a letter of agreement. In many cases, members of the corporation will even make sales calls with the consultant. When the project is completed, the corporation is dissolved.

The Stern approach also solves another dilemma that consultants used to face—what happens if a practitioner hires someone, and they run off with the business? Which often happened. You could not permit junior consultants or assistants to get "too friendly" with clients. There was the threat of the account executive stealing the client and opening his or her own office.

Generating "employees-at-will" without hiring, has enabled the independent consultant to increase profits in other ways. No longer do they have to spend dollars for an office in order to house employees and impress clients. Without the office and employees, the independent consultant has lower overhead, and almost without exception, can usually undercut the fees being charged by larger consulting corporations. With lower fees and consultants with equal or greater expertise, the entrepreneurial consultant can usually compete against rivals of any size.

Small Consulting Firm versus Large

Stern says "the typical large consulting firm has a huge infrastructure, and that has given us a pricing and profit edge in today's cost-conscious market. The playing field is level."

Lower fees do not mean lower profits. Novotny, for instance, operates out of her home, and with the reduced overhead she is generating a six-figure income. The same is true of virtually every other consultant in the top 10. Lower overhead and lower fees do not necessarily translate to lower net.

With the lower overhead, today's consultant is emulating their client companies. The clients have downsized to increase profits, and most independent consultants have done the same. Neither has a reason to bring on permanent employees. Both can get the job done with part-timers or freelance workers.

The client company's attitude has made a difference, too. The era of hiring the well-known consulting firm, that is, the practitioner company with the name, is gone. Today, the CEO, CFO, or whoever is doing the hiring is only interested in three things: qualifications, price, and results.

Clients also discovered something else—big name did not necessarily mean the consultant who handled the project would be well-experienced. In many cases, a senior partner came out to do the selling, and a junior executive did the work. With smaller, entrepreneurial firms, the principal does the selling—and the work. There isn't anyone else.

Branberg, who spent 15 years with Peat Marwick before opening his own office, saw there was a real opportunity for smaller firms to make inroads with major clients. He has taken advantage of that opening. Branberg has generated large corporate clients and has even presented proposals in several foreign countries, including the government of Latvia.

"It illustrates," he says, "two new elements in consulting—relationship marketing and a global economy. I didn't know anyone in Latvia, but I did know an attorney in San Francisco, who did some work for an investment firm in Houston. The Texas company owned 49 percent of the investment, and they were looking for someone to put together a marketing and business development strategy. My background with a major consulting firm helped, and the prospect knew it. The relationship paid off."

Novotny benefited from a similar connection. Before she opened her practice, she worked for a major hotel chain, providing sales training services. Her first client was the chain, which realized she could do the job whether she was employed by them or as an independent contractor. Others in the hotel field have realized the same thing about Novotny. She has the ability.

CONSULTANTS JOINING CORPORATIONS

One other factor has enabled these top 10 companies to compete successfully against major consulting firms. Some call it a blending of consultants and corporations.

Leggett explains, "During the past few years, a number of CEOs and other key executives, who once were consultants, went to work for corporations in key positions. Their expertise was such that the companies hired them. These people understand the consulting process, and they know that it does not matter whether you hire someone from a small or large company. They key is their expertise and qualifications."

Another difference between today and the 1980s, is "the role the consultant plays once they have come back to the client with solutions. In the old days," says Stern, "consultants frequently had an adversarial relationship within the client company. Employees hated to see them arrive. It usually meant that someone was going to lose his or her job. There was a natural opposition."

Today, it is different. With the shrinking workforce, employees are glad to see us arrive. They know management is not going to lay anyone off because it isn't possible to make further cuts. They recognize the consultant is their ally. Most important, when the practitioner develops a plan, employees are brought in and play a key role in implementing it.

Consultants do not just deliver a plan and leave. Management knows that nothing is going to work without the cooperation of the entire workforce.

Women as Consultants

Another major change is the emergence of women in the practitioner ranks. Men dominated consulting less than a decade ago, but in the 1990s, women have made significant inroads.

Part of the credit for this belongs to corporations. In the 1980s, companies developed programs that fostered the hiring of female executives. Although huge numbers of women entered the corporate ranks, many encountered the so-called "glass ceiling," that is, the imaginary corporate ceiling that prevents many women from advancing beyond a certain rung in the organizational ladder.

Although they had skills, many women were stymied in their companies. A growing number opted for leaving the corporate world and opening their own practice. Novotny and Needham left the corporate world. They found the only ceiling in place in consulting is the one the practitioner builds.

But, being an entrepreneur is not the same as working for a Fortune 500 company. The sensitivities differ. Novotny explains that "there is tremendous opportunity in owning your own business, however, you have to realize that when men and women interact there are going to be conversations that can be misconstrued. If someone— whether it is a man or woman—takes offense at everything said, they will not be in this business, or any business of their own, for long.

"Running a small consulting practice is quite different than being part of a large corporation. There is no human resource department to enter the picture, and it does not matter whether you are a man or woman. What counts is if you produce."

Needham believes female consultants have an advantage. "We have great instincts, and read people well. Women are super listeners, too. That gives us an edge because the ability to listen well is the difference between a good and bad consultant. Listening. If you can't do that, you'll never be a success."

Women Dominate Several Fields

Mirman has always been in a field dominated by women. "That's the nature of meeting planning and the hospitality industry. Meeting planners usually come from the hotel or hospitality industry, which is traditionally low-paying. Consequently, men shy away from it, especially if they are good in sales. For men, there are other sales jobs where they can make more."

Beekman goes beyond the men/women comparisons and says the thing that "we all appreciate is that it is liberating to be in charge of our own destiny."

In the next chapter, we will take a closer look at these 10 consultants, and the techniques they—and others—have used to launch their practices and create their own destiny.

CHAPTER 2

GETTING STARTED AND HOW THE 10 DID IT

It was a career that started almost by accident. For more than five years, Carol Beekman had been a French teacher in a public school. Then California beckoned. She decided to take a chance. She quit her job, and with her savings in hand she bought a one way ticket to California.

"I had wanted another career for a long time, something other than teaching," Beekman recalls. "I thought to myself, California is the land of opportunity, and if you want to make it this would be the place."

For consultants as well as others, California is indeed the land of opportunity. It ranks right alongside Florida, New York, and Hawaii as the place where more new ideas and business concepts are developed than anywhere else. It was California that first came up with computer stores and tune-up shops. Thus, for budding consultants like Beekman, there could not have been a better place.

NEED FOR BUSINESS PLAN

Beekman, however, did not just get up one day and decide to go into business. "I took more time than most people. I developed a business plan, talked to a financial advisor, other consultants, and friends. I wanted to make sure I was taking the right step. At the very least, I think a prospective consultant should put together a business plan. Figure out where your revenue is going to come from for the first year. Look at your prospective client base, and expenses. Regardless of whether you are entering communications/public relations or some other field, you have to ask—does it make sense?"

THE IMPORTANCE OF AGENCIES

Beekman had never been on her own. But, she had 20 years of experience in her field in the corporate world as well as with a consulting agency. Working with an agency was a distinct advantage. Aside from Beekman, six out of the top 10 consultants worked with agencies, and most credit at least a portion of their success and ability to deal with clients to it.

"Agencies are a great experience," says Beekman. "It is almost like being on your own. You have to pursue potential clients, do the work, put together reports, develop relationships, and solve problems. All the same things you would do as an independent consultant. The one difference—the agency is paying you a salary."

Every consultant knows that working with clients takes more than professional ability, it takes human relations and skill. Although executives leaving the corporate world and eyeing consulting as a career, usually have the skills to do the work, they frequently do not know how to handle clients. Or for that matter, generate business.

Dealing with a client is totally different than working with employees. In the latter, you are the boss first and what you say goes. In the latter, you are a listener first. Agency background helps in both areas.

"In many ways," says Beekman, "you become the client's confidant, and you have to be a good listener. You also have to be able to think rapidly and negotiate. Before you say something, think it out—carefully. It is always acceptable to a client to say something like 'let me think about that one' instead of blurting out a hastily conceived answer, and putting your foot in a hole. Clients take a great deal of what you say literally."

DIVERSE INDUSTRY EXPERIENCE ADVANTAGE

While with the agency, Beekman worked with a variety of industries—everything from banking and cosmetics to health care and insurance. Her philosophy was not to specialize in any one industry because "it narrows your prospects. In communications/public relations you can perform the same function for a variety of companies in different industries. I think that diverse industry experience was an advantage when I opened my practice."

Still, diversity can be a drawback. Even though a good, competent consultant can apply the same techniques to a variety of industries, clients believe that if you do not have experience in their industry, you may not be able to do the job. Thus, it takes selling skills, and an approach to show the prospective client that your abilities are, indeed, transferable to any industry.

Aside from client skills, Beekman is also fast-paced, and she likes doing "twelve different things on the same day." Beekman advises that one of the things that is critical for any consultant—regardless of the field—is to know the "prospective client's company . . . and know it well. Research before you ever make a call. Get brochures, sales literature, talk to secretaries, and even the operator who answers the telephone."

Without knowledge, consultants are at a disadvantage and, adds Beekman, "if you do not know something about the company, it sends a message to the prospect that you did not care enough about it to do some research before you made your call. If you are knowledgeable, you'll find the client will listen to you even more than they do to their own people."

THE FINANCIAL REWARDS

Running her own enterprise also made Beekman realize where the financial rewards were—"working for yourself." And she knows that first-hand. When she first moved to California, she was trying to break into the communications/public relations business, but she had the usual problems—no one is going to hire you without experience, but how do you get experience without someone hiring you?

Beekman did it the traditional way. She started at the bottom. Her first job paid anything but high wages—it was in Orange County, California, where she was hired ($4.50 per hour) as a part-time employee to handle the grand opening for a new cultural arts center.

"You have to remember," she smiles, "I was new to the field. I could write, and I had a good instinct when it came to promotion, but I did not have experience. I was lucky to be hired, even at $4.50 an hour." The week long grand opening went so well, that the city decided to retain the neophyte publicist full-time.

From there, Beekman moved from one job to another, all in the communication field, with each position offering more responsibility and involving her in a different industry—from government, cosmetics, health, to "you name it." Eventually, she wound up at an agency, and saw, first-hand, what it was like generating clients and working with them.

Beekman recommends agency experience for anyone thinking about consulting as a career. "Just to see how people generate billings and explain them to clients is important."

Beekman was hired by one of the largest real estate franchise organizations in the country, a multimillion dollar conglomerate that gave her the chance to meet her communication peers from coast-to-coast. These relationships were critical when she opened her own practice. She had built relationships with experienced professionals across the country. One of her initial clients came as a result of her meeting and getting to know another communication professional located 2,000 miles away, who needed Beekman's assistance with a client.

MEASURING OPPORTUNITY IN EVERY FIELD

Before she opened, however, Beekman posed the same questions to herself that every consultant has prior to taking the plunge. "Is there opportunity in my chosen field? Can I make it? I don't think you ever really know. You can have a hunch or feeling. Ultimately, you have to take a chance. But, have enough capital on hand to support yourself for a year."

As it turned out, Beekman's company was profitable from the day she opened her doors. It has been one of the fastest-growing operations in the industry ever since.

Her firm's rapid growth illustrates the opportunity in the communications/public relations field. It also shows one other point: Regardless of the amount of research you put into your industry, the only way you really know what is going to happen is when you actually open your doors.

Beekman's entry and rapid (less than 30 days) rise to profitability also illustrates the importance of selecting a profession that has opportunity. Gerry Stern's experience is similar. Before he opened his office, he had both agency and corporate background. He had dealt with clients from an inside and outside perspective, and knew the approach and skills that a consultant would need in order to prosper.

IMPORTANCE OF SELLING SKILLS

"When I look back," he says, "I was like a lot of other people. I knew a lot about reorganization, but knew little about consulting. But, when you think about it, if you are employed by a corporation, and you are in a position where you have to bring a project to your boss and sell him on it, you are consulting. You're selling."

"You sell external clients in a similar manner. Internal and external 'consulting' is the same. It involves the same selling process. You have to know the client (your boss or an external client) well. And, you have to know what they need, not what you want."

Stern spent more than 20 years in the corporate world with Fosco Corporation, where he was responsible for organization planning and compensation. He also spent time with Dart Industries and Hewitt Associates, a leading consulting firm.

In 1985, when he decided to open his own practice, he was far from being a stranger to the industry. "Most of my working life was spent in consulting," he says. His decision was not spur-of-the-moment either. "We (Stern and his wife, Yvette, who works with him) had been talking about consulting for several years. Frankly, we were looking for something that would be more fun and challenging than the corporate world. Consulting was it."

Stern says there are subtleties within the profession that determine whether you are going to be successful or not. Consultants have to read clients, and figure out one other important thing, "how much change can the client and the company tolerate. You have to be a communicator and psychologist. You have to be able to read the corporate culture. That is, what's going on in this company. You find that out through research."

Consultants Sell Twice

He cautions that some consultants have the tendency to try and fit client companies into a profile or category. "Don't. They do not always fit. Some are unique. Approach the project with an open mind.

"Consulting," he says, "can be a rewarding, lucrative field, but you have to convince clients not only to use your services, but your solutions as well. You are a salesperson. Think about this—you have to sell the client twice. Initially, you have to sell them on your services, and then you have to sell your solutions."

If there is one thing that opened the door for consultants such as Beekman, Stern, and others, it is the economy of the late 1980s and 1990s. It convinced most Chief Executive Officers that in order to survive they had to concentrate on what they did best. Manufacturers tossed aside dreams of building data processing and accounting departments, acquiring distribution centers, or other "synergistic" lines. They set their sights on one thing—producing a quality product, and to look outside, to the consultant, for such functions as technology assistance, human resources, accounting, and other services. This movement is not a fad. It is a trend that is impacting companies in the service as well as the manufacturing sector. It is no secret that these changes are responsible for the demise of many white and blue collar workers.

EXPLOSIVE GROWTH OF CONSULTING

But the door has swung both ways. A lean corporation still needs accountants, technology, training, and other support professionals, and most of those have come in the form of outsourcing—part-timers, temporary workers, and consultants.

Two industries—entrepreneurship and consulting—have exploded during this period. Fifteen years ago, *Entrepreneur Magazine* estimated that there were approximately five million potential entrepreneurs in the country. In other words, about five million people who were prime candidates for starting their own business. At the same time, the government pegged the number of small businesses, that is, those with 50 or less employees, at around 13 million. Today, those figures are dwarfed. Small business, including consulting practices, are booming. This boom is driven by factors that show no signs of slowing.

First, no one has a "job for life," and workers know it. Executives know if they are displaced at their company, there is not always going to be another equivalent slot waiting for them, regardless of experience.

Couple this with the enormous number of immigrants entering the country—workers who usually find their greatest opportunity in "doing their own thing"—and it becomes apparent as to why consulting practices and small business ownerships have exploded.

Business opportunity shows, which were once held sporadically and seldom in markets other than the large, metropolitan cities, are commonplace. Almost every week, there is a "start your own business expo" that can be found in some major city.

For every manufacturer who closed its technology department, there is a technology consultant who has found a client. For every organization that has cut its field trainers, there is a training consultant who has found a client. For every human resource department that has downsized and laid off its compensation professional, a compensation consultant has found a client.

SPOTTING CONSULTING DEMAND

Interestingly, not one of the consultants in this book did any special research into their 10 diverse professions before opening their doors. Beekman did a business plan, but none of them actually spent time doing market research to see if they could survive once they opened. They could see the demand.

In the 1980s, before consultants entered a field, they did market studies, interviews, and assessments. There is little of that today, which is evidence of the abundance of opportunities. For the most part, there isn't a consulting field that takes research and guesswork. Every one of them looks good.

Compensation consultants such as Andrea Needham have seen the opportunities grow rapidly. "It is not only the fact that human resource departments are short-handed, but they are also encountering new demands from employees who survived downsizing and remain with the company. Many of those demands revolve around compensation and adjusting it."

When Needham started in the business, compensation was based on how many people and departments reported to a manager. The more departments, the more dollars. It was simple.

Today, companies realize that the employee who has direct contact with customers—regardless of whether they are an hourly employee or a highly paid vice president—are all equally as important. Because of this new view, compensation is no longer simple. It takes an experienced, creative professional to answer wage, salary, and benefit questions, and develop sensible plans for the future.

"Compensation means more than just salary," says Needham. "How are you going to structure something that not only keeps your top people, but gets them to work harder than ever? Compensation is one way to help solve the problem." It is a giant problem—and one that has created enormous demand for consultants such as Needham.

Needham, a native of New Zealand, has more than 20 years experience in the compensation field. Once again, experience is critical. "I think," she says, "we are going through—and will continue to do so—a restructuring of the world's economy. The information age is here, and the turmoil in companies is going to be here for a generation."

LOOKING TO THE FUTURE

"For compensation and other consultants, this is a time of opportunity. It has never been like this before. You have to look into the future. Think about it. Regardless of what your background happens to be, your profession is going to be impacted by the changes we are going through. Change scares many people, but for astute professionals it represents opportunity. There is going to be demand for a host of consulting services, not just mine. You just have to use a little vision."

Needham is especially excited about the prospects for compensation consulting, and even "if you do not have the background or experience, you can get it. Get into the field. Work for an agency as an apprentice. Follow a senior consultant around. Whether you have the skills or not, the opportunity is here."

Business Is Changing

Needham did what she advises. She studied consulting techniques in America, as well as Europe and Asia. She knows how the business is changing. Some change is being driven by technology, others by restructuring, and still others by what Needham describes as risk.

"When you think about it," she explains, "most executives in the United States today are not paid to take risks. If they do, and they fail, they are out. They avoid risks. It is the employees who are on the front lines, dealing with customers. Companies see this and they want to restructure their pay systems. That is going to create more opportunity in my field. It will also generate additional business for consultants in dozens of other professions."

The demand that Needham sees in compensation, is similar to what Cindy Novotny has encountered in sales training. Sales is the heart of every business, and although Novotny struggled during her first year, today she is in the six-figure income bracket and providing services to companies worldwide.

Novotny's story is the epitome of success. She left a secure, safe job as a trainer for a major hotel chain, and opened her doors. She did not have any clients, only the support of her husband, who agreed that he would provide funding for a year.

Trading Title for Opportunity

"When I started," she recalls, "I did not have any qualms about making it. I left a great job, where I was one of 65 directors in the company. I was one of only three females who had that title. I had tremendous opportunity with the company—a great job—and title.

"For many, that would be a turn-on, but not for me. I did not care about fringe benefits, company car, or any of that stuff. I wanted to be on my own. I did not want to go through any more political agendas or hear office gossip. I like to say what's on my mind, and opening my own business gave me that opportunity."

Novotny's comments bring up another important element in determining success. Consultants have to be driven. They have to be willing to give up the corporate trappings and, if need be, struggle. They also need the drive that Novotny has displayed. She runs a disciplined, structured operation, "and never forgets to sell. Regardless of how much business you have, you better always be looking for more."

Novotny's first account was not enough to pay the groceries. "But, I worked out of my house, kept my overhead low, and got my business cards, telephone, and typewriter (I could not afford a computer). And, I kept plugging away. I made a deal with my husband that I would keep at it for a year. If I made it, fine. If not, I would do something else."

Learning Never Ends

At the beginning, Novotny admits she did not have a plan . . . only enthusiasm and drive. Novotny believes that consultants should never stop learning. Many open their practice; they have 10 or 20 years in the field, and "they believe they know enough. I don't think you ever know enough."

Novotny reads every business book she can get her hands on. At least one a month because she is "scared to death I am not going to know what's going on out there. That I am going to miss something." Novotny believes consultants must keep on top of things. She cites *The Wall Street Journal* as a must and then laughs about it. "When I was in the corporate world as an employee, I never read anything. Now I don't miss anything."

If there has been a secret to Novotny's success, it is her drive. Her schedule is more demanding than any other consultant's in this book. She travels 50 weeks out of the year, usually Sunday through Thursday. On Friday, she comes home and leaves again Sunday night. Her travels take her to every part of the world. She has trained in places ranging from mainland China and Europe to Palm Springs.

Novotny knows her schedule is as busy as it can get. "I'm 38 years old, and I do not want to keep this pace my entire life. If I do it now, for a few years, I won't have to. Now, I have the opportunity."

Consultants as Entrepreneurs

Novotny looks upon the successful consultant as an "entrepreneur, not a small businessperson. There is a difference between the two. A lot of people want to be an entrepreneur, and they believe that owning their own business will make them one. Owning a print shop does not make you an entrepreneur. It makes you a businessperson."

"That's radically different from an entrepreneur; the difference is that the businessperson may still be thinking like a corporate person; someone who works for a company. But, an entrepreneur does not. An entrepreneur thinks about the challenge and the creativity of doing your own thing. They do not care about the company or the corporate trappings.

"Successful entrepreneurs—and consultants—get up in the morning and are driven by the desire to make their enterprise a success. If they are like me, their heart pounds, and there is excitement when you start working. If you think that way and get stimulated whenever you think about business, you are ready to open your own consulting practice."

Rudy Dew's excitement level matches Novotny's when he talks about outplacement. An outgoing, gregarious businessman, Dew smiles and says "I cannot believe I have a job that pays me to socialize. Sure, I have to do marketing, but I get to socialize with some exciting people. I enjoy marketing, training, and technology. Those are the key ingredients to this business."

Dew says if you have a tendency toward those three factors, you can be enormously successful in outplacement. You also have to like people, and if you do, this is a "business that can work anywhere."

It is also a business that Dew admits he almost left before he got started. It happened with his first client, an executive who had been laid off. Dew was retained to counsel him. The executive, who was an officer of the company, was so shaken when he was laid off that he could not drive. "I drove him home. I felt bad. It is a crushing experience to see someone go through a layoff or firing. Even though it was not happening to me, it impacted me to such an extent that I almost quit the business."

Overcoming Obstacles

Dew stuck to it. That's a trait that is a necessity in any consulting field. "We frequently get disappointing news. Maybe it is a client you did not get, or a project you are handling that the client is not happy about. It happens. But, if you are going to be a success in this business, you have to pick yourself up and keep right on going. That's what makes the difference between successful and unsuccessful consultants."

Mike Green is accustomed to picking himself up. When he launched his management consulting practice, he made telephone calls and sent hundreds of letters out at a time. Rejection was not unknown to him. Still, it did not discourage him and he is quick to say, "I am not a salesman, and I never thought of myself as one. However, in every field there is a certain amount of selling required. You have to use the telephone or write letters when you are getting started because there is no referral business. Referrals only come after you've been in the business and done projects. So, initially, you are going to have to make calls. The key is not to let the 'no's' or 'I don't need you now' get you down."

Once a client is generated, Green says one critical thing for every consultant to remember is how important it is "to be able to handle people gently. Never in a threatening manner. Our success depends on information, and you will never get any if there is intimidation. You cannot be pushy in this business."

Green lives his advice. He is easygoing and soft-spoken. He feels at home dealing with clients, and perhaps that is because he has been doing it for years. "The more you do the better you get." Still, he has seen both good and bad times in the profession. Today, it borders on the "best" and appears to be getting even better.

The Quality Emphasis

Green says one thing that has opened up his field and created more demand, is the emphasis on quality that is sweeping companies throughout the United States. Numerous consultants have carved a special niche in that area alone.

"Every company, whether it is manufacturing or service, is searching for improved quality. Most of the time they come to management or quality consultants to develop programs." One quality program that created an enormous demand was Total Quality Management (TQM) which was a buzzword for a long time in many industries. Companies such as AT&T paid millions of dollars to consultants to examine existing quality procedures and design new ones.

"While TQM has certainly created demand for consultants," says Green, "ISO 9000, a quality procedure that took root in Europe, has become the rage, especially with manufacturers."

Emergence of ISO 9000

ISO 9000 started in England and was adopted by the Common Market in the mid- to late-1980s. The procedure is simple: Workers write down how they do things, whether it be manufacturing or service. The way they describe the process is the way things should be done.

Auditors take the written procedures and follow the workers as the process is actually being done. If the process varies from the written, employees (and the auditors) quickly discover the differences, and the company has to fix the "nonconformance." Often, in getting the process back to a conforming state, quality is upgraded.

"The standards," says Green, "are not long. It can work with any business or industry, and it has become so highly regarded that many companies will not deal with suppliers unless they have gone through ISO 9000. The quality demand is certainly one of the major factors driving this consulting area."

FOUR KEYS TO SUCCESS

Green's keys to success are: (1) experience, (2) knowledge, (3) competence, and (4) a good sense of humor. Those elements work in management, as well as every other consulting field. Green's experience includes nearly 14 years in industry as an industrial engineer and manager of several companies before opening his management consulting doors more than six years ago.

Green is a relationship builder. He is a member of the Institute of Management Consultants, an umbrella consulting organization that does not hand out memberships easily. To become certified, a consultant has to submit written summaries on their last five consulting jobs, and the Institute calls each of the clients to "grade" the practitioner before certification is given.

Brad Leggett is another consultant who has benefited from years of experience. He worked for Burroughs and got his selling experience by selling mainframe computers, and working on accounts ranging from Lockheed to NASA. He did international marketing (Asia) and was sales manager for a technology company before opening his practice.

Leggett has an unusual twist to his background. He is involved in two industries—high tech and credit unions, which are seemingly wide apart. Leggett, however, has background in both.

In high tech, he works with firms in helping them determine their direction, market, and approach. He looks at channels of distribution and the viability of different sales lines. He is a valuable commodity in today's competitive marketplace.

His second industry, however, is unique. He works with credit unions, and helps them with the same marketing problems. "Working with credit unions may seem unusual, however, I have been dealing with them since my days at Burroughs. I sold them financial products, and while doing so I could see they had a real sales and marketing need. I put it in the back of my mind, and decided to work in that industry when I opened my practice."

Leggett's practice has boomed. Companies have trimmed sales and marketing people, but getting products into distribution (and the customer's hands) is more difficult than ever.

There is another reason for Leggett's success. He has a background in sales and does not hesitate prospecting or looking for new clients. Although he believes in building relationships, Leggett knows that the backbone of any consulting practice is sales.

Focus on One Segment

When he opened, his initial projects came through the relationships he had built. And he targeted his sales efforts to one area of sales—industrial. Leggett is a firm believer in using a rifle instead of a shotgun. "Don't be all over the lot. Focus on one segment of the market and hone in on it. Become a specialist and develop that kind of reputation. Generalists have a much more difficult time in building a practice."

Leggett is organized and disciplined, as is Jack Branberg, who calls his consulting "strategic alliance" or "strategic development." Branberg is the epitome of consulting experience and education. His father was in the military, and the family traveled the world. Eventually, Branberg earned a Bachelor of Science and Finance degree from the University of Minnesota, and an MBA in finance.

But degrees do not necessarily make a good practitioner. Branberg learned the trade by doing it for others. He spent more than three years with Ross Perot's company EDS, where he headed the firm's West Coast consulting operation and "identified opportunities" for the company. Being able to recognize opportunities, that is, prospective clients, has been a driving force behind Branberg's success.

After leaving EDS, he joined Peat, Marwick as a partner and spent 15 years with them and ran the general consulting group in Los Angeles. Three years ago, he retired from Peat, Marwick and opened his own practice.

Branberg's background of working with major corporations has played a key role in his success, as well as the type of clientele he has today. He has built relationships with top Chief Executive Officers throughout corporate America, and his skills are known internationally as well as domestically.

Even with that background, Branberg had to go out and sell his services, just as every other consultant does. he credits his client base to relationship marketing, which he believes is the strongest marketing tool available to today's consultants.

Referrals—Where They Come From

Branberg says the launching of his practice was probably different than most. He left his previous job on a Friday, and opened for business on Monday. He had no clients, "but on the second day a referral called. Ironically, it was my old firm that called. It was a market research project, and something they did not do."

Branberg's corporate experience has given him additional insight into clients, and what they seek when they contact a consultant. "It is only natural to think of selling when you meet a prospective client, but remember that in this business you will never do well if you try to 'sell' your services. In consulting, we are marketing a service. Clients are sophisticated, they don't care about lunches, and they do not care about brochures. When you meet a prospective client, think about them—think about what they worry about when they are in the shower. If you can anticipate their concerns, the business will be there."

Branberg's "strategic alliance"/"strategic development" practice could be called marketing because he focuses on three things: (1) how to generate more revenue from present clients, (2) how to better serve clients, and (3) how to generate future clients.

Based on those concepts, Branberg developed a practice that focused on where he thought clients were going. "You have to be able to see ahead—to forecast in this business. For several years," he explains, "we've seen clients focus on expense reduction. Now we are trying to help them generate more revenue. We look at their current mix of products and services, as well as the company's infrastructure. We assess the company internally, and look at its customers, too. Then we come up with a plan to increase sales and better serve customers."

Companies typically call in Branberg when they want either to introduce a new product; increase sales per employee; want to assess the possibilities of entering new markets; or when they are thinking of acquiring another company and divesting some of its products, or merging with another firm.

GREY HAIR IS IN

Those diverse projects call for a variety of highly skilled abilities. Branberg likes to say that "grey hair is in. Companies want to work with consultants who have the knowledge. They do not want to hire a rookie, and watch the person learn on their time. Fees are not the problem. A consultant has to 'walk the talk.' They have to deliver."

To help him deliver, Jack has gathered a consortium of 10 top former CEOs as "senior consultants." They are not paid employees, but they work with Jack in making presentations and solving problems. He hires them on a project basis. Thus, Branberg is utilizing the technique that others have found highly desirable—bring in outsiders and utilize them on a part-time or project basis.

"When you can say to a client, 'I can bring with me a group of senior people who have done all this before. People who have lived through and handled similar problems. They come in and hit the ground running. There is no learning curve—on your time,' they are impressed."

With that approach, Branberg has found that companies, which once only focused on cost control, have now stepped back and want to generate real growth with real earnings. "Today, they are looking at consulting firms to help them get there."

While nearly every consultant in this book carefully planned their practice and how they were going to handle it, there is an exception—Laurie Mirman. Laurie was working for Kelley services as a branch manager. She had been in the industry for nearly six years, and decided she wanted to get into something that looked like it might be more fun—"the hotel business."

One problem: She did not have any experience, and no one would hire her. Ultimately, Laurie's persistence paid off. She landed a job with a small resort hotel, made the hotel one of the most in-demand properties in the area, and parlayed that into a meeting planning practice.

BUILDING THROUGH COLD CALLS

Laurie, like Cindy Novotny, knows the importance of sales, especially to a new consulting firm with minimal connections. She built her business the hard way—through cold calls.

"I know that approach sends chills through some people, but if you want it bad enough, you can do it without any relationships or connections. I started without any leads, and built this business. But, every day I cold called . . . and even today, despite the fact we will handle more than 600 meetings this year, I still cold call. In every consulting practice, you have to sell. That might be through cold-calling, letters to previous clients, letters and calls to referrals, or relationship marketing. Whatever technique is utilized, it has to be done on a regular basis. That's what makes your company successful."

Mirman is now in the process of expanding her business. While site planners specialize in booking and negotiating hotels and meeting rooms, meeting planners go one step beyond. The planner can do everything from working with the hotel to arranging banquets, meetings for the group, special decorations, and even helping to design a theme for the meeting/convention.

It will take Mirman's company to a new level and present additional challenges, however, she says "we were doing extremely well with site selection, but I needed a new challenge . . . I love cold-calling, and I wanted to do something more. This is it."

Needham believes female consultants have an advantage. "We have great instincts, and read people well. Women are super listeners, too. That gives us an edge because the ability to listen well is the difference between a good and bad consultant. Listening. If you cannot do that, you will never be a success."

WOMEN DOMINATE SEVERAL FIELDS

Although Needham's field has its share of women, Mirman's is dominated by females. "That's the nature of the meeting planning and the hospitality industry. Meeting planners usually enter this field after they have spent time in the hospitality industry. It's a good training ground, but it does have disadvantages."

One of those is that it is low-paying. Consequently, men shy away from it, which is one reason why it is dominated by women. Gender aside, it is an excellent training ground for anyone interested in meeting planning. The hospitality industry gives them the chance to become familiar with hotels, an entity they have to bargain with for their clients, and with future prospective clients—the companies and executives that are visiting and renting hotel space.

Regardless of the consulting industry someone enters, a practitioner can count on facing one thing—pressure. "It is not the same kind we faced when we were with companies," explains Stern. "The consultant's pressure is typified by the need to satisfy clients, pay the bills, meet deadlines, and, of course, generate new business."

When it comes to building business, consultants have a dual challenge. There have been many laid-off executives who donned a consulting hat in hopes of earning something while looking for a new position. Numerous clients were burned by the part-timers, and it has made prospects wary of hiring anyone who is pursuing their trade part-time.

Thus, it is difficult to try and launch a practice without being committed full-time. Companies have become more discerning. They have smaller budgets, and for the most part, only want to deal with consultants who are in it for "real."

LOW START-UP, HIGH PROFIT

For those serious about entering the profession, the financial promise is enormous. Even better is the investment required. Low cost opportunity is present in nearly every one of these fields.

The majority of consultants can hang out their shingle for under $5,000. In some cases, $1,000 will do. Typical equipment is a telephone, fax, computer, and laser printer. Contrast this with the enormous expenditure that consultants had to make in the 1980s for secretaries, expensive office suites, and other high-priced launching necessities.

Still, not every consultant can get away for $5,000 or less. Dew is an exception. He has 30 computers, which clients use for researching firms and industries that may be able to offer them a position. Aside from hardware and software, his rent was high, too. He opened in downtown Los Angeles, because he thought the number of corporations located there would be beneficial.

Dew quickly discovered that although companies were there, the unemployed executives he would be working with, lived elsewhere. After he generated contracts from several corporations for his outplacement services, he found the unemployed executives he was supposed to serve, were at a disadvantage. They did not live downtown, yet they had to drive or take a bus to his office. Parking fees were high as well.

Dew recognized the problem and leased an office in the suburbs that was close to two freeway interchanges. Easy to get to, no parking fees, and it had the office environment he sought.

A home-based business would not work for Mirman, either. Her staff has grown to 10, and they are on the telephone constantly selling. She needs space.

Regardless of where the consultant locates, the returns can be phenomenal in today's market. Every one of these 10 fields has enabled their practitioners to generate six-figure incomes, with gross profits of 30 percent or more.

Novotny says sales trainers can easily gross $500,000 "even if you are not dedicated. Contrast that with the jobs we came from," she says excitedly. "Maybe we made $40,000 to $60,000 with a 2 percent annual raise. That's not much comparison."

Nearly all consultants can work out of their homes, and the biggest overhead expenditure is usually telephone. It does not take much to set up a home office, and clients do not care. They know a fancy, high-rise suite is going to be reflected in higher invoices.

Despite the high profit and low overhead, starting is not easy. There is business, but consultants have to develop clientele, and that takes time. A back-up of six months savings is advised, although many consultants are in the black within 30 to 60 days.

NEED FOR MENTAL TOUGHNESS

Consultants also need mental toughness. Good salespeople have it, and anyone who experiences adversity on a daily basis and survives to come back, has it.

An important part of the consultant—and any business—is selling. During the course of the sales process the consultant is going to get many negatives. That can be distracting and discouraging "especially if you are working alone with no one to bounce ideas off of," says Stern. "This can be a roller coaster business when it comes to emotions. We've all had our down days."

Leggett agrees. The way you think means a lot. You need "tenacity as well as sales ability . . . the ability to stick to it."

Organization and discipline are two additional traits that run through each of these 10 professions. Working alone is not easy. Working alone from your home can be tougher. There is a temptation to get up later, drink coffee, read the newspaper before you do anything, and mix household chores with business. "When you operate out of your home, you need a schedule and you need to stick to it," says Novotny. "Even when you don't operate out of your home, you need discipline, a format, and a schedule," echoes Mirman.

Both Novotny and Mirman's stories show what can be done by someone who has no clients to begin with but a ton of determination and discipline. Dan Potter's story is similar. Potter, whose primary focus is executive search for the health care industry, entered the profession about eight years ago as a recruiter for an agency.

"I learned the business from the bottom up. My first involvement took me to the financial industry, where I worked with banks and savings & loans in finding employees. Although I was not thrilled with the industry, I learned a great deal about the philosophy of how to do a search. How to be a headhunter."

LEARN FROM OTHERS

Potter's point is that prospective consultants should find a place to learn their industries. Work with companies, learn the ins and outs of the business. Aside from the industry and companies, prospective consultants have opportunities to learn from others, too. Successful consultants frequently are willing to answer questions and give advice. Ask consultants in your field. Although some may not be willing to give the time, most would.

Potter did exactly that. He talked to a headhunter who had started a practice similar to the one he was thinking about. The prime difference between the two was that Potter was going to specialize in one field, while the other, established consultant was doing searches for companies in a variety of industries.

Potter learned it and liked it. "Executive search is a business for someone who wants to see a project started and completed. Then you go on to the next project. You get great satisfaction from it."

Potter's motivation in going into business was similar to many other practitioners and businesspeople. He not only wanted to do his own thing, but he wanted to be compensated on the basis of how well he performed. That does not always happen at the corporate level. However, before he could put his plan together, his wife went into early labor at six and a half months. That's when Potter made a decision.

With his wife flat on her back per doctor's orders, Potter left his company, and went home to help his wife take care of the house. For three months, he stayed home. Even after the baby was born, Potter stayed. "It was something I will never forget. I had the opportunity to let my daughter know who her father was."

At the same time, Potter started calling people for whom he had worked. He wanted to get a reaction to what people thought, since his idea was new to the industry. It was Potter's way of doing market research. The question was would they be willing to utilize his consulting services, if his cost for conducting an executive employment search was based on a "menu of possible services" that he had put together. The client could hire him to do the entire search and interview, or just a portion of it. The positive reaction he received convinced him he had a winning idea.

Thus, Potter Associates, executive search firm, opened less than 18 months ago. From the day he launched his practice, Potter's enterprise has been profitable. In fact, at times he shakes his head in disbelief at how rapidly the company has grown.

NEED TO INTERVIEW AND ASK

There is more to success, however, than having a good idea. Potter says to establish a good consulting practice in the search industry, you have to "have excellent interviewing skills, and be able to ask probing questions. You can get something from every call you make—if you ask the right questions. That's what search is all about—questioning.

"When I opened, I wanted to build a small, niche search firm. I did not think beyond the first six months, and had enough capital to cover my costs.

"I knew I could do it. Frankly, I think anyone who has faith and belief can make it in this business, too. You need two things—discipline and determination." As part of the discipline, every consultant has a routine. They get to the office about 8 A.M., and it does not matter whether the office is in a high-rise office building (Mirman) or at home. Several even wear a coat and tie to the "office."

Working at home can pose a problem, especially if a client decides to visit and bring several associates along. Beekman has it solved. She has made arrangements with an associate who has a conference room available if she needs it for a meeting. If there is a conflict and someone else is using the room, she will rent one. "The nice thing about this business," smiles Beekman, "is that you could run a practice from Alaska. Location does not matter."

Green is walking proof of Beekman's statement. He can usually be found near the beach area in southern California, walking in shorts and casual shirt with loafers. Of course, when he sees a client, he wears a coat and tie.

Needham says "image used to be everything. It is still important, however, what compensation clients want to know more than anything is 'can you do the work'? We can. That's one of the reasons our firm—and small consulting enterprises like ours—have not only been able to compete with the large consulting firms, but we've been able to knock their brains out."

CHAPTER 3

THE MARKETING STEPS—FROM PROSPECTING TO RELATIONSHIP MARKETING

Nearly every industry has been impacted by economic uncertainties, however, if there is one thing that is certain it is the continuing need for consulting services—regardless of industry.

Take, for instance, the real estate industry. A few years ago, there were more than 800,000 agents nationwide, companies were prospering and even part-time agents were doing well.

Sales trainers, computer operators, accountants, and other support staff for agents found themselves with more business than they could handle. Then the Recession of the late 1980s hit. Interest rates went up, down, up, down, and the ranks of agents began to thin drastically. From 800,000, the number of salespeople dropped closer to 600,000, and as the numbers dwindled, companies began to cutback and layoff trainers, CPAs, and technology people.

But, a funny thing happened. Although the ranks of the agents thinned, the total number of home sales remained high. In fact, in

1993 and 1994, sales were at an all-time high. What was happening? If sales remained high, why were so many agents leaving the industry?

The answer was simple—the lion's share of home sales was going to a smaller percentage of salespeople. In every industry, there is an 80–20 rule; that is, 80 percent of the sales are made by 20 percent of the salespeople. The same was true for real estate, but in the late 1980s, the rule began to tilt even further. Some industry analysts estimate that 90 percent of the sales are being made by 10 percent of the agents.

Regardless of the exact figures, one thing appears evident: Less agents are making more sales, and the ranks of the salespeople are being thinned. The marginal producers are being weeded out. That's happening in all industries.

DOWNSIZED COMPANIES NEED HELP

Despite the drastic restructuring, companies still need to supply the top-performing agents with high quality sales and marketing training. Managers need good management training courses. Accountants are still needed to monitor sales and commissions. And technology people are needed to develop and service hardware and software programs that will make the agents even more productive.

That is why consulting—whether the industry is real estate, hotels, or automobiles—is thriving and will continue to do so. But how does the consultant reach these prospective clients? Through marketing.

For any consultant to have a winning business, they have to spend time marketing. Some consultants spend as much as 30 percent of every day pursuing new business, or trying to generate additional business from previous clients.

PLATE FULL SYNDROME

True, referrals are an ideal source of business, but referrals are slow to come to the neophyte consultant. Even consultants who have an abundance of clients, know the importance of marketing on an ongoing basis.

Mike Green says "the tendency is to slack off when you have a full plate. When business is good, we forget marketing. Then, all of a sudden, your client base dwindles and you jump back on the marketing program."

Although Green jokes about his tendency to slack off, he and the other nine consultants in this book, are some of the best marketers in the business. It is part of their daily routine. As Laurie Mirman says, "not a day goes by that I do not make cold calls." Cindy Novotny has the same mental set, and every consultant—whether they be in the business or just thinking about it—has to think marketing and be disciplined when it comes to pursuing business.

The most common marketing mistake consultants make is forgetting to keep in touch with clients after the job is done. Client follow-up and contact is one of the most important elements in any marketing plan.

Client Follow-Up—What's Involved

For years, mail order firms have proven the value of previous customers and the importance of keeping "in touch" with them. Studies show that as much as 50 percent of additional business can be generated from a present client—if contact is maintained.

On its simplest level, the retail clothier who sells a $250 suit to a customer, can generate at least another $125 in sales from the same person—if they keep contact with them. The key is keeping your name in front of the client.

In the real estate field, successful salespeople do monthly (or quarterly) follow-up letters. They send notes, make telephone calls, and even knock on the client's door. The idea—keep your name in front of the prospect.

Consultants have the same opportunity. Some do newsletters, however, Andrea Needham cautions that the "newsletter should have quality content. In compensation—as well as any field—if you cannot put a newsletter out that people want to read, do not put one out at all."

Needham put out a regular edition that she mailed to present and prospective clients. It always revolved around compensation, and covered some of the new, innovative pay techniques that companies were using. She targeted the mailing to human resource directors, CEOs that she knew, and her client base. Needham eventually gave it up because "I just got too busy to find the right content, and I would not put it out otherwise."

FIVE MARKETING METHODS

Needham and other consultants have five possible marketing contact methods they usually follow:

1. *Referral*—Its impact is usually felt once the consultant has a practice that has been operating for six months or more.
2. *Prospecting*—A must for every newcomer.
3. *Cold calls*—A must for every newcomer.
4. *Follow-up*—A key to generating referrals.
5. *Vendor assistance*—A practice that both new and old consulting firms should be looking into.

But, how do you get started? How do you generate that first customer? How did these 10 consultants do it?

For Laurie Mirman the answer was simple—"cold calling. I just got on the telephone and called every possible person. It's old fashioned, but it works, especially when you have to pay the rent."

Targeting

Mirman did not just make random calls, however. She targeted. Every consultant should be targeting. Where is your market? Who are they? How do you reach them? Should it be by telephone? Is there a better method? What about one-on-one? Is there a place to meet them?

Mirman knew her market. First, she called associations across the United States. "Associations host many meetings. For example, the American Medical Association is one. There is hardly an association going that does not host at least one a year. I simply called them.

And, if they did not have one upcoming, I asked about their membership. Did they know of any of the members—that is, any member companies—that were planning to have a meeting or convention?"

Rehearse First

If you use the telephone, have a good idea of what you are going to say. Mirman says "I feel comfortable on the telephone, but other people do not. If you feel awkward, prepare a script and practice." That's exactly what telephone marketing firms do. They practice.

Not every prospect is going to give the consultant the opportunity to follow the script verbatim, but it provides a guide. "The other thing," says Novotny, "is be sincere and know what you are talking about."

"Make sure you are speaking to the right person, too," adds Mirman. "I always ask 'who is responsible for coordinating your conferences or meetings?' It could be a meeting planner or secretary. Never assume."

Mirman says that to market effectively consultants should have a "good sense" of what the other person is like on the other end of the line. "Make sure you are calling at a good time. Ask. If the person sounds as if they are rushed, ask if there might be a more convenient time to call."

NEED FOR BROCHURE

Calling does not mean you have to make a sale with every conversation. Often, the call is the first step in introducing your services to the company and or prospect. The call also enables consultants to learn more about the client and the way they operate.

Rudy Dew smiles when he thinks of the telephone. "When I started, I called everyone I knew. Every human resource professional in the business. I let them know I was in business. For many, I had to explain outplacement, so I decided to put together a brochure. The problem with brochures is that unless someone needs the service right then, they just throw it away."

"The telephone was my best vehicle. One thing to keep in mind. Not everyone knows you are in business. You have to tell them. It is surprising when you discover how many people who do not know you are in business, and the percentage of those people who can bring you business."

Cindy Novotny used the telephone extensively, and she still does. Initially, she called prospects in her industry (hotel), to see if they needed any sales training. She also used the telephone to break into other industries, a tactic that has enabled her to generate almost 40 percent of her revenue from corporations other than those in the hotel industry.

"I generated my largest client through the telephone. I called them every quarter for four years, but finally I broke through . . . they were ready for a sales trainer. If I had not called on a regular basis, it would never have happened."

SELLING WITHOUT PRESSURE

Mirman says many people have the misconception that you have to be high pressure on the telephone. "That is not true." She points out that there are few clients who can be generated by this technique.

"High pressure does not get you anywhere," she says, "regardless of the consulting field. People buy things when they have all the information they need. The purpose of every telephone call I make is to inform and educate." Education, she says, leads to the sale.

Mirman and several of the other consultants, do not stop with telephone calls. Mirman follows her calls with notes, making the person she talked to aware—once again—of her firm. If any of the associations was planning a meeting, but it was a year or so away, Minar pends the name and number.

Pending files—although they sound basic—are important. Mirman, calls her's a "tickler" file. She pends client's (associations or companies) name and number on a certain date. When the date comes up, she makes a follow-up call.

Although Mirman has several thousand client names in her database, she has an "extraordinary memory and I might just think of someone out of the blue and call them. I know the ones who are active, too. I make sure if we have a client with an upcoming event (they can be scheduled several years in advance), we call at least six months before the date to see if anything has changed."

Several consultants do the same as Mirman, only they take it a step beyond. For instance, if they get a name and number, they send a note to the person on a bimonthly or monthly basis. The note may simply say:

> Dear _____,
>
> Thought you would like to know we just held a meeting for the (name of company or association) at the (name of hall/hotel) in (city). There are some interesting new facilities at the (name), that I thought you might be interested in seeing. I've enclosed a brochure on the facility. If I can supply any other information, please let me know.

This note leaves the door open for the consultant to follow up. They do not have to wait for the prospect. It also gives the prospect something of value—a floorplan, brochure, or other information. Something they may use in their meeting planning. Whenever a note is sent, the goal should be to supply the recipient with something of value; something they can use.

Clippings with Notes

There are variations of this technique that consultants use. Some watch the daily newspaper (or tradepapers) and if they see anything pertaining to a client, their company, the industry, they clip it and send along with another note.

> Dear _____,
>
> Thought you might be interested in the enclosed. Hope all's going well.
>
> Sincerely,

Mirman's company does this on a regular basis. "But," she cautions, "if you do not have anything of value to send, don't send it. Don't waste the client's time."

Andrea Needham uses both mail and the telephone. She calls previous clients, and has an assistant who does mailings on a regular basis to 200 CEOs. She also sent a quarterly newsletter, but does not put one together (a one-pager) unless there is something of "interest for the client."

Rudy Dew maintains contacts with law firms. Companies that are contemplating layoffs, usually contact attorneys beforehand to check into the liability they may run into. Often they ask the firm for an outplacement recommendation, and Dew's name surfaces because of the relationship he maintains and his problem-solving ability.

If you are doing any kind of client program, "don't forget the people who may not be clients but have direct contact with them—like attorneys," says Dew. The same is true for other consulting practices.

Beekman works with companies in the communications/public relations area, however, there are other departments within a company that could recommend her services; departments ranging from advertising to sales and marketing.

Jack Branberg sends a unique note. It represents a significant investment, but is extremely effective. He sits down and develops ideas for a former client or prospect. He even brings in a designer, has them illustrate the idea, and he puts it together in a professional presentation. Then he sends the package, along with a note to the prospect. It is impressive.

The client has not asked for the ideas, but when they come across the desk they cannot help but notice the professionalism and the work that went into it. "It makes an impact," says Branberg, "and even if they are not interested in our services at the time, it shows we care enough about them to go to an extraordinary expense. I don't think anyone else in the industry goes to that extent."

They don't. And, although it is a significant investment and a crapshoot, it makes an enormous impression on the prospect.

"If the client was even thinking along those lines, we have a good chance of getting them to sit down and talk about the concept in greater depth. It is a door opener."

CASUAL TELEPHONE CALLS

Branberg does not always send something elaborate. "At times, I will just call a client, tell him I have an idea, and ask if they have some time to discuss it. If they do, I'll stop by and give them two or three ideas; ideas I formulated specifically for their company, at no cost. I might do that two or three times with a former client, and never charge. It shows the client you are thinking of them and that the consulting fee is not the only thing on your mind."

DIRECT MAIL IMPACT

Branberg is not a fan of direct mail. To him, it is too impersonal. "If you get a letter from Jack Branberg, you probably do not know who I am. There is no 'brand name' recognition. But if you get something from Price Waterhouse, you recognize the name, read it, and you might retain it. For the independent consultant, I don't think blanket mailings are effective. I prefer giving something customized to the prospect . . . something I have created especially for his company."

Not all consultants agree with Branberg when it comes to mailings. Mike Green probably sends more mail than any consultant. His mailings—as many as 500 at a time—are not customized for any one firm, and in that respect he differs from Branberg, Mirman, and others. Still, he gets results.

"My feeling," he explains, "is that a consultant only gets hired when the client needs you . . . when they have a specific job in mind. If they get a mailing piece from your firm, and they do not have a need, they will just throw it out. But, if your mailer hits just at the time they are beginning to think of a project, or know of a problem— bingo. You are in."

PROACTIVE MARKETING

Branberg calls his technique "proactive marketing. I come up with crazy ideas and/or approaches and send them. It shows the prospect or client our creativity and gives them a reason to hire us. It works with strategic alliance, and I think it would have a positive impact in any field. It shows your ability, and the fact you know your business, and the client's."

Gerry Stern's marketing approach is as creative as Branberg's. A few years ago, he had an idea and decided to publish a book, a book that would have appeal and be in demand by every one of his potential clients. He calls it the "Stern SourceFinder." It is an in-depth reference book loaded with information for human resource departments. It has become a Bible in the industry, as well as a tremendous lead generator.

The "SourceFinder" runs more than 500 pages and is used by human resource (HR) people to find out about the latest laws and changes in the HR field. An HR director can pick it up and find information on everything from discrimination to health and safety.

Book as Marketing Tool

Originally, Stern produced the book as a resource for his company, since it was doing a tremendous amount of reorganization work with HR departments. He discovered it was a superior marketing tool, that could be left with clients. "There is nothing that we could have put together that would have left a more positive impression," says Stern.

Three years ago, Stern put out the first edition and now he is into the second printing. The second printing is expanded and covers a number of topics that are hot buttons when it comes to human resources—sales compensation, motivation, reorganization, and how you diagnose and analyze a company.

The first edition took Stern four years to put together and "it is not something we readily give out. For example, if it looks like we are really going somewhere with one of our proposals, we may give it. It lets the prospective client know that we are well-rounded in human resources. When we want to make an impression, there is nothing better."

The book has established Stern as the authority in the reorganization field, and he credits much of his referral business (80 percent of his clients are referred) to the impact of the Sourcebook.

BENEFITS OF PROFESSIONAL GROUPS

Branberg says his entire marketing approach is designed to build relationships. He builds relationships wherever possible. But, he does not join groups just to build relationships. There are numerous organizations that he has joined purely to help improve his area. He did not become a member to enhance his practice.

"If you get into a civic group with the express idea of building your business, I think it is a mistake. People sense your motives and it will not pay off."

Branberg is not talking about trade associations or industry groups. For example, he belongs to the Orange County World Trade Association, and he is on the Board of Directors of a group called Partnership 2010. Both groups are looking to the future and trying to make the community a better place in which to live.

Mirman belongs to several meeting planning groups, but says she has not had time to attend any of the meetings.

"I'm too busy making calls, although I do believe that industry trade groups would be a definite benefit for most consultants. Aside from building relationships, you have the benefit of hearing about new developments and techniques."

Green belongs to several professional groups, including an association of professional consultants, as well as an international management consulting group. He sees two prime benefits. First, when you are a sole practitioner, and you are running a business without anyone else in the office, "it gets lonely and you can lose touch. It also gives you the opportunity to exchange ideas, see what's happening and see if fees are changing."

REFERRALS

The most potent form of marketing in consulting is referral. This is where relationship marketing impacts. If someone knows you—and is familiar with your abilities—there is an opportunity for a referral.

Andrea Needham says referral works in her industry, "but only on the West Coast." Her feeling is the East is more formalized, and prospective clients are going to visit a "name" firm, whereas on the West the name does not matter as much as the referral.

The best initial referral source is the present or past client. But there are others. Needham, for instance, cites the importance of belonging to professional organizations.

"Aside from the other consultants you meet, membership in professional organizations make clients feel good, confident. For instance, I belong to the ACA, a compensation/consulting organization. When you put that on your letterhead, it gives you additional credibility."

Dew belongs to the American Association of Outplacement Professionals, an international organization that meets once a year. Professionals come from every state and foreign countries, and Dew says it is valuable from several perspectives. "First, it is a marketing tool. You meet people, build relationships with them. Oftentimes, they may have a lead for a client that is not in their area, but your's. Additionally, you find out what's happening in the industry. New trends."

RELATIONSHIPS ARE KEY

In launching a practice, Branberg constantly stresses that the key marketing ingredient is relationships. "You have to build them long before you ever go out on your own. People need to know you are professional, highly skilled and ethical. They will never learn that at a chamber mixer."

Relationships should be built before a consultant opens an office, and the building should continue long after the practitioner's shingle has been hung. Branberg has enormous contacts/relationships, and he developed them over a period of years with Peat Marwick and others. When he opened his doors, they were waiting.

"Frankly," he recalls, "I expected to be in the black the first month. I know that sounds egotistical, but my situation differed slightly from others. Remember, I had been consulting for 15 years while I was with Peat. I knew how to deal with clients, and I understood what they expected. Although I did not have a client when I opened, by the second day I had a call that led to one."

Branberg has built his business entirely through relationships. "I know it sounds simplistic, but there are a large network of people that I have over the years. I have done many projects, and the success of those jobs is the best marketing tool a consultant can have. Your past performance is going to dictate your future revenue."

Thanks to the relationships he has built with clients and other professionals, Branberg can handle a number of assignments at one time. By himself he is limited, however, he has a network of temporary workers, and there is almost no limit to what he can do.

Although newcomers to the consulting ranks may not have the contacts of a Branberg, his techniques are worth noting. Building relationships has paid off for him and every other consultant. Needham, for instance, has used relationships effectively. For 10 years, she has had her own practice and, as is the case with Branberg, she had clients from the day she opened.

"They knew me from my days with McKinsey. And they had the opportunity to judge my work. It was not as if they were buying something they did not know about."

Needham concurs with Branberg's assessment—"this is a relationship business. You have to build. It may take time, but word spreads." One client tells another.

INDUSTRY GROUPS

Another marketing tool utilized by consultants is industry groups. Needham joined the ACA (American Consulting Association) and met people. Although some of those in the organization may be viewed as competitors, they are "great sources of information and business." On many occasions, one consultant will refer another to a job because they may be too busy. Or, perhaps the project involves expertise they do not have. "They cannot refer you if they do not know who you are and what kind of work you do. Join," says Needham.

As previously mentioned, Needham feels there is a difference in generating clients from East Coast to West Coast. West Coast clients, she feels, are generated by consultants primarily because of the "trust and relationship the consultant has built with the client."

Marketing on the East Coast is more formalized. They buy the firm and the process. "That's why most of the big consulting firms have been successful in the East, but they have been unable to obtain a substantial foothold in the West."

Stern built his practice much the same way as Needham and Branberg—relationship marketing. His first consulting job was with a former client. "We were about to open when a consultant I used to work with approached and without my asking, he jotted down a list of names and numbers. His comment was that they might be people who could hire us. We contacted the names, and from the list we generated our first client. You cannot underestimate the importance of relationships."

Relationship marketing enabled Beekman to launch her company and register a profit within the first 90 days. "Before I got into communications/PR, I talked to numerous of people who were in business. They gave me excellent advice."

Then, a fellow communications consultant she had met, called her and asked if she was interested in splitting an account. The client required different services, and Beekman could offer some of them, the other consultant the rest. They split the account and she was on the way.

"One thing I found," she recalls, "is there is a big difference between saying you are going to go into business, and actually taking the plunge." Many prospective consultants talk about it, but never open an office. Consequently, prospects always remain prospects.

"You must make the commitment. Sure, I was worried at first, but as soon as I did take the step, I found business. Clients want to deal with serious, full-time consultants."

Beekman did what many others have done to market services. She went through her rolodex, plucked out every name she could find that might have some influence, and sent announcement cards to them. "From that one mailing I generated enough business to keep me busy for a year."

The point that Beekman and others drive home is the relationship, and the fact people do not know you are in business until you tell them.

Rudy Dew built his initial relationships in the outplacement field four years before he opened his practice. He started when he opened the Hay Group's (a consulting firm he worked for) first outplacement office in Los Angeles in 1981.

Outplacement was new, and even Dew says, "I did not know what it was." Aside from the consulting acquaintances he built, Dew also constructed a solid relationship with human resource directors, and he developed a marketing campaign designed to appeal to his most important customer—the human resource director.

"Many people misunderstand relationships. It is not networking, it is faith-building. Think of it as a sales process. When you sell something, the buyer will not commit unless they are fully informed and have faith in the seller. People will not recommend you unless they feel comfortable about the recommendation." It is impressive to have a consultant in the industry recommend you. The second type of person that Dew builds relationships with is prospects. "I built my marketing campaign around those two principles. Make good contacts in the consulting field, and in human resources."

To reach the people in human resources, Dew developed an educational approach. He supplied them with information; information that helped them do a better job. The information came in the form of clippings of informative articles (which he sent along with a short note to the HR directors); a newsletter, trade show contacts, and "no obligation" advice.

Dew scoured publications to see if there were any articles pertaining to outsourcing or the HR function that might be of interest. He cut articles out, duplicated them, and sent them along with a note to the HR directors he had on a list.

The note never asked for business, but it showed the HR professionals that Dew's company knew what was going on in the industry. And, he built a relationship—through the mail.

Dew's newsletter had articles that "were never self-serving. They were educational. We tried to give the HR director something they could use. It had good, solid information."

At industry trade shows, Dew had the opportunity to get "one-on-one" with HR directors. Dan Potter does the same thing, and has since he opened his office 18 months ago. It has proven to be an excellent source of contacts for prospective clients. Dew liked the trade shows because they enabled him to meet people who did not normally get out of their office.

"In our field there is an association of outplacement profession-als. They meet once a year. Couple this with the many HR trade shows, regional and national, and you have some excellent market-ing opportunities."

Dew's final marketing tactic was advice, free advice (similar to Jack Branberg's approach). "I might hear about a company that is about to go through a downsize, move or close a plant. I would call and offer some no-obligation consulting. When we opened in 1985, outplacement was still foreign to many HR people, and they wel-comed our assistance. Even today, there are many firms that appre-ciate the advice. Our network has grown such that now the HR departments call us before we call them."

Leggett did target marketing, too. He focused on industrial sales and initially his first client came from someone he had met in a civic organization to which he belonged. In the long run, however, he found that targeting a small niche in industry was most effective.

TARGETING WITH DIRECT MAIL

Leggett put together a simple, tri-fold brochure, and had two sales letters as follow-up. They kept his name in front of the industry, and helped—however, he says in the long run it was the "relationships that brought him business."

Leggett did several other things, too. He keeps his eyes and ears open, and if there is an opportunity or connection that someone he knows needs, he tries to help. "It may not involve me, I just try to be of assistance. More than once, I have put two people together, and months later one of them came back and I got some business from it. What goes around comes around. Especially in a service business like consulting."

Mike Green's direct mail campaign has probably been more in-tense than most. In fact, he built his practice with it, and developed a tactic that others can emulate. First, he targeted his market—small businesses that ranged anywhere from $1 million to $50 million.

Next, he targeted specific companies, manufacturers that he found in the California Manufacturer's Register. He went down the list, studied each company, the description, and picked out those that he thought would fit his services. (His background was industrial engineering.)

Green plucked a couple of hundred companies at a time. His package consisted of a brief, one-page letter that had his accomplishments in bulleted format ("almost like a resume"). The letter was always personally addressed to the president or chairman of the board. He never used labels, either. The name and address was always on the envelope.

Although most mail order experts recommend telephone follow-up for maximum effectiveness, Green did not do any. "I know everyone says you should, but I have a different theory, and I think I have proven it. Regardless of your qualifications, you are not going to get called unless there is a need. Think about the things you get in the mail. The solicitations. You discard all of them unless you happen to hit a flyer or letter that is selling something you need."

Green's mailings are sent in anticipation that a CEO will open one when they have a need. "If they do, I have a good chance of being called and getting the project." As evidence, Green cites a recent client he signed who called him directly after a mailing. The client failed to remember any previous mailings by Green, although the consultant had sent the same person four other letters.

"My approach may not be the most scientific, but I believe—and I think other consultants would agree—that we are not going to get hired unless there is a need. The key is to have your name in front of the decision maker when that need arises.

"If I send out 500 letters, and get one-half of one percent return, I will generate two to three clients. The other advantage of the mailing system is that seldom will you compete against anyone else. If my letter hits the CEO when he has a need, I will get the call. The company will not call two or three others for competing bids. Today, things are not done that way."

What Green does with direct mail, Cindy Novotny does with the telephone. When she opened, each day she made cold calls to hotels to see what their sales training program was like, and if they needed help. Eighty percent of the calls she made were to hotels, because that was the industry she knew.

Novotny knew something else. Sales training is used by more than one industry, which is one reason why it is such a hot, rapidly growing profession. "I did not want to base the success of my business on one industry, when my skills were transferable. I could do sales training in a variety of industries, so why not call them?"

It is easier to call people you know, and Novotny knew the hotel field. Still, she forced herself to make at least five calls a day to people who were not in the hotel field. These calls differed from the approach she used with hotels.

"I knew the hotel business and most of the companies in it. But I did not know anything about some of these other businesses I was calling. Before I talked to the person in charge of training, I found out about the company." All consultants should be doing the same thing. Making cold calls without knowing anything about the prospective client is a mistake, and usually a waste of time. If you don't have any idea as to how they operate, you will never be able to ask the questions that lead to an appointment and eventually the business.

Novotny talked to anyone who answered, and asked questions. "Does your company go to any particular firm for its training? Do you use an outside trainer? I got information from everyone, even the operator."

Eventually, Novotny worked her way into the sales department and asked questions about their training. She talked to Human Resources, too, because even though HR does not usually do the hiring, they are normally involved in the process when a decision is made to utilize an outside trainer.

"That decision usually comes from the vice president of sales or marketing. You never want to snub HR, because even though they do not make the final decision, they can impact it. Get someone on your wrong side, and you lose."

Novotny seldom did. With perseverance and discipline—not to mention daily telephone calls—nearly 40 percent of her sales training clients are nonhotel, and the percentage is growing. Typical of the success of her stick-to-it attitude, was her dealings with a hotel chain that is considered among the top three quality hospitality chains in the country.

From the day she opened, she called. Each time, the vice president of sales thanked her, but declined the services. Every quarter she made the same call, and every three months the answer was the same. In between the telephone calls, she wrote notes, reminding the vice president that "Master Connections," the name of her company, was there.

For four years, the process continued with negative results. Then it happened. The vice president moved on and the new executive saw one of her letters, just as he was ready to outsource the hotel's training. He called, gave her two weeks to prepare a presentation, and she flew to Florida to meet him and other officers of the company. She presented her proposal, and got the job.

The case illustrates several things. First, you have to be persistent. Consultants must go through a regular sales and marketing routine daily. Marketing your consulting practice does not take a sales whiz. It does, however, take persistence and discipline. Stick to it and you will get your share of the business.

Consultants also have to be knowledgeable. Novotny knew the hotel and its training needs well. When the call came and she only had two weeks to prepare, it was not a problem. She had made a study of the chain, and knew the ins and outs. Without knowledge, it is impossible to present a proposal that is going to win. Novotny had the knowledge.

Because a client is a major corporation, such as the hotel chain, that does not mean they want a major consulting firm to handle their training. The prospective client wants to see and know the person they are going to be dealing with; the person to whom they will give the business.

Clients do not like to crawl through layers of consultants. That's an edge that Novotny and other practitioners with limited staff have. They not only make the presentations, but they do the job, too. What the client sees, they get.

Novotny was not the only consultant who started without a client base. Mirman did the same, and she had little difficulty in building her practice. "I do not let a day go by without making sales calls. I think that is a mind set that every consultant needs. Sales is the lifeblood of our business. If you forget that, you might as well forget consulting."

BUSINESS FROM SUPPLIERS

Making telephone calls and using direct mail are marketing techniques that are utilized by most consultants, however, there are other innovative sales approaches that are not commonly known—yet they work.

One is what Branberg calls "backward integration," a potent marketing tool that can lead to business. The term has several meanings. First, a consultant might have a client who is actually a supplier for another company that is also a potential client.

For example, suppose Branberg, or one of the other consultants, was doing business with an aerospace company that was supplying parts to Boeing. The consultant might ask the aerospace client to introduce them to someone at Boeing, which would be called "forward integration."

Another possibility would be if the consultant was doing business with Boeing (the client). They could ask Boeing to introduce them to someone at the aerospace company who was supplying Boeing with parts. That's "backward integration." Either way, the relationships can provide the basis for a potent marketing tool.

A similar opportunity is building a relationship with suppliers who are providing services to prospective clients. The supplier may not be a client nor is the prospect, but the supplier can help open the door for the consultant. There are few who know more about what companies are doing (or planning) than vendors and/or suppliers. They usually have contact with purchasing and other departments within the firm.

MAINTAINING LISTS

Green maintains a list with 50 suppliers on it. He stays in touch with about half of those via the telephone and has generated several consulting jobs through their input. "They know," he says, "what's happening."

Leggett offers a word of caution with vendor arrangements, however. "When you come in to see a client, you want to be neutral. You do not want to endorse a (vendor's) product, simply because he opened the door for you. That's the only caveat I have with vendors and utilizing them to market your services."

Green, as well as some of the others, have developed arrangements with other consultants. For example, he works with one consultant who "loves to sell clients" but does not like doing the project. The two worked an agreement where one sells, Green does the work, and the fee is split.

BUSINESS FROM SUCCESSFUL COMPANIES

Green offers another word of advice to prospective consultants—business will come from the ranks of successful companies. "Typically, companies that hire consultants are usually the ones that are doing well. Companies that are doing poorly rarely allocate the funds, and cannot afford consulting services most of the time."

SHOULD YOU ADVERTISE?

While building relationships, direct mail, telemarketing, joining organizations, and "backward integration," all lead to business, one marketing technique that receives lukewarm (at best) reception from successful consultants is advertising.

"It does not pay," says Green and those sentiments are echoed by others. Advertising is designed to sway opinions and produce a preference, and it works well for products and some services that do massive, repetitive advertising. But, for a personal service that depends on relationships, advertising is a waste.

It is one thing to sell toothpaste and McDonald's hamburgers to the masses, but executives of major companies are generally more sophisticated than the mass market. They want the best person for the project, and emotion rarely sways them.

If advertising does not work, what does? And why do consultants such as Green recommend that 30 percent of a practitioner's time should be spent "marketing themselves?"

What works for some is keeping in contact, building relationships with people you have done business with in the past, and promoting yourself whenever and wherever possible. Public relations or public-ity works. Community relations/volunteerism works—if you are sin-cere. As Branberg notes, people can spot a phoney in a minute, and if you have volunteered solely with the hope of generating business, people will know; they will read it.

The Cost-Effective Business Builder

Consultants agree, the most cost-effective manner to generate busi-ness is through referrals, which are built through relationships. An-other way to build relationships is through marketing techniques such as seminars, public relations, and direct mail.

Seminars are a valuable tool for the consultant who knows the market and how to reach the prospects within it. For instance, Leggett gives seminars to credit unions on marketing. It sets him up as an authority, and someone who knows how to expand market share. Most of those in the audience are not qualified to conduct the marketing activity themselves, but if they like what they hear, the consultant who is giving the session has a good chance of turning a prospect into a client.

SPEAKING AS MARKETING TOOL

Leggett says an overlooked marketing opportunity is speaking. Whether it be in front of an industry organization, or a prospective client's company, the exposure and credibility has impact.

"The advantage," he says, "is that speakers are regarded as au-thorities. They generate respect, and that helps build relationships and business." Leggett, however, says that speakers sometimes stray from the subject and talk about things that do not interest the audi-ence. Every speaker should be aware of "the audience, what their in-terests are, and what their needs happen to be. Speaking should never be looked upon as an opportunity to hard-sell, either.

"If the speaker does a good job, he is selling himself. If he does not, he may be turning everyone off." Leggett recommends studying the audience carefully. "Know who they are. Develop a topic that will involve them, emotionally if possible."

Leggett targets his talks to prospective clients, and always makes it a point to give them something in the talk that will help them with their business. Something of value. It might be describing a new, money-saving technique or process, but every talk should be built to give something to the audience. Good solid information.

Branberg gives talks, too. Usually, his subject is sales and marketing and the global marketplace, topics on which he provides consulting services.

Beekman, an accomplished speaker, gives talks revolving around how "PR can help the bottom line of your business" and "why CEOs should be paying more attention to PR." Both topics obviously are targeted at owners, the people who can retain Beekman.

Needham loves speaking and has only recently got into it. Although she is a trainer and accustomed to being in front of an audience, speaking at a podium was different.

Novotny admits she did not begin giving formal speeches until a year or so ago. One of her salespeople not only sold a client on Novotny's training expertise, but convinced the client that the sales trainer was a pro at the podium. As a result, the client booked Novotny to present the keynote address for a professional conference. Since that time, she has expanded her topics, and today she gives talks on such topics as "stress in the retail environment," a talk which she spent countless hours preparing. "I ended up talking to 25 retail managers at Anne Taylor stores so I could find out exactly how they felt, and how stress impacted them. By the time I gave the talk, I had first-hand experience and felt confident about the message I was delivering."

Novotny's point is that if you are a trainer, consultant, or salesperson, beware—speaking in front of a group differs from giving a sales training presentation, talking to a group of executives at a board meeting, or selling a project. Novotny says "it takes totally different skills. It takes rehearsal and timing. Speaking in front of a group for an hour is totally different than conducting a training session for the same amount of time. In training you have interaction; at the podium, there is none."

Beekman, who has done talks for a number of associations and organizations such as the International Franchise Association, says that talks invariably leads to business. At the least, it will generate "additional contacts with whom you can start to build a relationship." Beekman does not wait, however, for associations and groups to call. She actively pursues them and makes calls on a regular basis as part of her marketing activities.

CO-SPONSORED SEMINARS AS MARKETING TOOL

Branberg does co-sponsored seminars, where he will speak on things that prospective clients are anxious to hear about—global marketing, reenginnering, new avenues of opportunity. The co-sponsors are usually trade associations, which have credibility.

The co-sponsoring approach is common in many industries. For instance, there are numerous ways that real estate agents try to reach first-time buyers. They know if they invite the buyers to a session, they will be looked upon with suspicion. The buyer knows their motivation—sell something. So, agents have gone to title companies and home mortgage companies to co-sponsor the sessions. The agent becomes part of the seminar, not the star. The buyer views the session with less suspicion, because it is being put on by someone who usually does not have a property in inventory that they are trying to unload.

Do Not Hype

Don't try and hype your services. Seminars that are used for hyping fall flat. Use the speech or seminar to help people, educate them, and show them how knowledgeable you are on the subject. Display that well, and the talk is bound to lead to a contact and ultimately a client.

PUBLICITY

Seminars and speeches are ideal for consultants to take advantage of another marketing area—public relations or publicity. Several of the

10 consultants utilize PR to promote appearances. They send news releases to the media that reach their market.

For example, if Branberg were speaking in front of a group of CEOs on "global marketing and the opportunity it presents for companies in the computer chip field," there are several business-building things he could do with a news release. First, he would want other CEOs (in the computer chip field—his potential clients) to know about the talk and his expertise. He could reach them through the business pages of newspapers, as well as through "trade papers" that go to the computer chip industry.

Where to Send News Releases

Thus, recipients of the news release would be (1) business editors of the local newspapers and (2) editors of computer (chip) journals. Typically, the release should be sent at least two weeks in advance. Although most newspapers can print material that is given to them the day before the event, waiting that long with a "soft news" item is a mistake.

"Soft" news is news that can be printed at any time by the publication. Contrast this with "hard news," such as crimes or election results which have to be printed immediately, or it becomes old news. Editors prefer soft news as far in advance as possible. That way, they have the option of putting in the release a week before the event or a day before it. Usually, it will be inserted when the editor has space. That is, when the ads and hard news leave a few holes. It is best to send the item two weeks in front.

Value of Trade Papers

A second possible placement for the release is the "trades." In the United States, there are more than 15,000 trades (industries) and each has publications that cater to people in those trades. For instance, there are numerous publications that go to people involved in the automotive business—owners of new car agencies, companies that manufacture parts for automobiles, and so on. If a consultant's customers are in the automotive field, he can reach them by placing a news release in the automotive trade papers.

If Branberg is trying to reach computer chip manufacturers, there are numerous (computer) journals that go to people involved in the field. Once again, the release should be structured and sent to editors of trade papers.

A word of caution, however, when it comes to trades: Some are published daily, weekly, others biweekly, and still others, monthly. Before sending anything, find out the deadlines. That is, if Branberg is giving a talk August 15, and the computer publication is distributed August 22, it is a waste of time, paper, and postage to mention the talk in this publication. The best way to determine deadlines is call the editor.

If you are trying to reach consumers through the business page of the local newspaper, call the paper and find out who the business editor happens to be. Send them the release, and address it to them by name. Why? Personalization.

Editors get hundreds, sometimes a thousand, releases every day. It is not uncommon for a local television channel to have 300 to 400 news releases faxed in one day. How do you improve your odds? Through personalization. Take time to call and find out the name of the editor. Address it to them by name, and try to avoid using mailing labels. Have the name and address printed directly on the envelope.

Getting Free Exposure

There are local trades, too. Most chambers of commerce have a newsletter. Don't forget them, because aside from chamber members there are scores of other business prospects who do not belong to the chamber that may read the newsletter when it is passed on to them by a member.

How can a consultant compile a media list? The chamber usually has one, and there is a second source—Bacon's Publicity Checker, a handy, fact-filled guide that will give you the names, addresses and telephone numbers of every trade paper in the United States, as well as every consumer newspaper and magazine.

Bacon's, which can also be found in many libraries, has several directories. Newspapers, magazines (trades and consumer publications), television, radio, and even syndicated columnists. Bacon's also gives you the name of the editor(s), however, these people change frequently, and it is wise to call instead of using the name in the book. (You'll find typical releases on seminars and other events in this book.) News releases are not long, detailed documents with flowery quotes. They are a basic selling tool and contain only the facts: who, what, when, where, and why.

Aside from the facts, if a consultant were sending a release about a talk they were giving, they could cull one or two key points (quotes) from the speech, and insert it in the release. The media is always looking for hot topics; topics that are of such interest that editors may go beyond a news release and assign a reporter (or TV crew) to interview you. Topics that are "hot buttons" and may spark an interview include consumerism, surveys, interest rates, and how other countries may be impacting our economy, either for good or bad. Pick up any newspaper on any day, and you will get an insight into the topics that are current. If a consultant builds his release around one of them, they have a greater chance of additional media exposure.

Generating Media Interest

Suppose, for instance, that a consultant was about to give a talk to a group of executives in the computer chip business about foreign competition, what to expect and why one country is about to become a prime competitor to the U.S. companies. This speech/talk has implications beyond the industry itself, because the increased competition may mean a loss of jobs, and a loss of jobs impacts everyone. Structured correctly, this release could spark media interest, and generate interviews for the consultant. While some consultants use this approach, others use a release that gives the results of a "forecast" or "survey," two additional topics which intrigue the media.

For example, Mirman could send one relating to the increased number of meetings being scheduled by corporations, and she could quote one or two company officials in it. It would show increased activity in meeting planning, because companies are more active and possibly more optimistic about the economy. When it is printed, it also mentions Mirman's firm as the meeting planner that is dealing with these companies.

Aside from being printed, releases of this type interest editors. In some cases, they may prompt the editor to assign a reporter to do an interview. The process that should be used when sending a release:

- Send it.
- After four or five days, call the editor(s) to see if they received it. The telephone call (which should not last longer than about 30 seconds, remember the editor is busy), is an opportunity for the consultant to briefly reiterate the topic in the release. To "soft sell" it.
- If the release appears, follow up with a thank you.

FREE TELEVISION EXPOSURE

When it comes to television, a consultant should use judgment. Television needs something visual. If you have something to illustrate the talk or speech and make it more entertaining, there is a chance of coverage of the event or a pre-event interview. The topic, however, has to impact the masses. That's where "unemployment," "rising prices and interest rates," and similar topics take precedence.

Some television stations have "specialized reporters," that is, reporters who cover a certain beat. For several years, business and the economy has been of prime concern to consumers, and a you will find television stations that have "financial reporters." These specialists look for stories that will impact the masses. A good financial/business story, built around a speech, talk, survey or seminar, can often lead to an in-depth interview.

To make sure all media see the release, many cities and communities have so-called "news services" or "business wires." That is, releases are sent to these services, and they handle dissemination. In some cases, there may be a charge, however, a "city news service"—

one that will put all newsworthy releases on it and electronically distribute to all media—is usually free.

THE TALK SHOW OPPORTUNITY

Another growing outlet is radio and television talk shows. There is an abundance of them in every market, and they are constantly searching for good, solid material that will interest listeners and viewers. Naturally, a trade story that impacts a small industry is going to be harder to sell than a story that impacts an entire community. If you can show how the small industry will affect all consumers in the market, you will have a much greater chance of selling it.

GETTING MILEAGE FROM PUBLICITY

Once printed, astute consultants "merchandise" their publicity. That is, they cut out, paste up, and reprint positive stories and send it along with a note to present and potential clients. Nothing has more credibility than the media. We tend to believe what we see, read, and hear.

Local media does not have the same muscle, but it does have impact. It can help consultants sell. The consultant who utilizes the free, positive exposure they have obtained is one step ahead of their competitors. Even television offers the opportunity to "merchandise." Several consultants utilize copies of interviews they have had, and they use it in client presentations. Once again, few things are more impacting. Typically, what most consultants do is get a copy of the story and send it with a simple note to the prospect. The story does the selling.

Even consultants who do not want to spend the time writing a release, have found ways to use the media. By visiting a local college (and sometimes even a local high school journalism department), they have been able to obtain the services of a talented, young, inexpensive student/writer. The student gathers the information and pens the release, thus saving the consultant writing time.

In some cities, consultants have hired freelance copywriters or public relations people to write releases. It is even possible to retain a professional PR person on a project basis. All this depends on the consultant's budget.

SUMMARY

Marketing is critical to every business, but consultants have a distinct advantage over traditional businesses such as retailers and manufacturers who have to spend thousands—tens of thousands—of dollars to make their story known.

To some, marketing is sales, however, Branberg puts it this way, "We are marketing a service, and if we try to sell our services in the traditional way, we will not get far. Consultants have to use innovative techniques, and some take time. But, in the long run, they all pay off."

CHAPTER 4

HOW TO DEAL WITH CLIENTS— THE NEW ATTITUDES

It started as if it would be a coup for communication's consultant Henry Adler, but instead it turned into a disaster. Most practitioners in the communications field remember it well. It began one sunny, summer afternoon following a long, presentation that Adler was making. The service company listened intently, and finally decided. The company had a serious problem, and after hearing from Adler about the work he had done with other firms that had similar image problems, it hired him. The marketing vice president notified Adler of the choice, but it was the CEO who made the final decision.

At first, the consultant/client relationship seemed ideal. Adler showed an excellent understanding of the company, its structure, and the problems it had. The firm's prime interest was to generate positive publicity in the local media. The company was pursuing a large government contract, and the entity that would award the pact was headquartered in the same city as the service company.

Although the firm had been in the city for years, it had never thought about the importance of positive publicity, and the role it might play in dealing with prospective clients, such as the government. Then, the city fathers announced the contract, a $23 million plum that the service company anxiously eyed.

But the government wanted to do more than just hire a company for the job. The mayor had expressed an interest in a company that was involved with the city; a company that cared about it. Adler's client had never shown any of these tendencies, that is, until the bidding process and the requirements were announced.

Adler was hired for a quick fix. The president told him to "get us some positive media exposure. Make us known to the government." Adler spent two weeks doing research on the company, and finally he came up with an idea; an idea that would generate the exposure the client needed.

With the idea in mind, he approached the business editor of the largest newspaper in the city, and sold him on doing a story. Adler was ecstatic. The only thing remaining was to bring the CEO together with the editor. That's when problems began to emerge.

For two weeks, the editor was too busy to tackle the project. Adler waited patiently. Finally, the editor told Adler he would not be able to do the story, but he would assign a reporter to the feature. Adler, seeing the story coming closer to fruition, excitedly notified his client. All they had to do was wait, it was only a matter of time before the reporter would call and set a time for the interview.

Time, however, dragged on. On several occasions, Adler called the reporter to see if he could facilitate matters. As it turned out the reporter was busy, too. But, he told Adler he would get to his client—soon.

In the meantime, the CEO grew impatient. He knew the newspaper wanted to do the story, and it perturbed him that the editor did not deem it important enough to conduct the interview himself. He was upset even more when Adler told him the reporter was tied up, and it would be several days, if not weeks, before he called for an interview.

Early one morning, four weeks after the reporter was assigned the feature, he called Adler and told him he was ready. In fact, if he could get the president downtown that day, he would do the interview in his office and have the pictures taken there as well. Adler was excited. He could see his weeks of patient work coming to a head. He told the reporter he would check with the CEO and get back to him within a few hours.

Adler called the CEO and was told the president was in a meeting. He explained to the CEO's secretary the nature of the call, and the urgency. She agreed and said she would have the CEO call him as soon as possible.

Two hours passed and Adler's impatience grew. He called the CEO again, this time explaining to the secretary where the interview would be held, and the fact he needed the CEO downtown that day. She told him she understood and would get back to him.

Adler waited as the tension grew. It was nearly noon, and he knew if he did not meet the reporter, the story could be delayed weeks. Perhaps even long enough to the point where it might not be written and published before the city government awarded the contract. He tried the secretary once more and was astounded at the answer. She had told the CEO about the call, but the president informed her that he could not go downtown that day. He had a prior lunch appointment, and a meeting with several of his senior managers that afternoon. There was no time.

Adler pushed the issue. Did the CEO understand what was happening? Did he know this was going to be the interview and from that the reporter would write the story? Did he know the reporter wanted photographs taken downtown? The secretary told him he did, but he did not have the time. In desperation and not wanting to lose the chance to position his client as a community leader, Adler asked if there was anyone else that the CEO would recommend to do the interview. The secretary did not know. Adler did.

Adler remembered the senior vice president, Fred Miller. Miller could do the interview as well as the president. He called Miller, explained the situation, and asked if he might be available. Miller was reluctant. It was the president's job, and he did not want to speak for him. Adler pressed. He told him how important it was and explained that the company might not get another chance for weeks, perhaps months. Miller said he would check with the CEO.

A half-hour later Miller called back and said the CEO, although disturbed that the newspaper had not given him more notice, had agreed to letting Miller do the interview. He was too busy for it.

Happily, Adler called the reporter and arranged the interview. That afternoon, he and the Miller drove downtown, the interview was conducted, pictures were taken, the story was written, and within two weeks the feature ran on page one of the Sunday business section.

Adler was beside himself with joy, as were most of the executives at the client company. That is, all but one, the CEO.

A week later, Adler received a letter in the mail severing his services, and two weeks after that the senior vice president was transferred from the corporate offices to a branch 2,000 miles away, where his duties were downgraded.

What happened? Every consultant knows the answer. Adler (not his true name) had committed the unpardonable sin—he had bruised the CEO's ego. The CEO was angry at the newspaper for keeping him waiting, and he was even more disturbed when the paper called at the last minute for an interview. Apparently, the reporter and editor did not realize how big his company was and how far in advance he planned. (The luncheon appointment the CEO had did not pertain to business. It was with an old friend, and could have been postponed, but the CEO chose not to cancel.)

Despite his years in the business, Adler forgot something; something that successful consultants never forget. Every client has an ego. Regardless of what they say, never underestimate its size or what can happen if a client has it bruised. Egos are frequently thought of as belonging primarily to those in entertainment or politics—celebrities. That is not the case. There is no shortage of self-esteem in the business world, and the consultant who fails to remember that fact can lose out much as Adler did.

Other communication consultants in Adler's position might simply have canceled the interview. It would have been safer, and although the story would not have run, the consultant would have retained the account. Adler and others are not being paid to assuage egos, but that may be part of getting the job done. When it does, the consultant may have to make a choice. Getting the project done in a satisfactory manner is one thing. Dealing with clients is another.

THE EGO FACTOR

The Adler story happened several years ago, and although consulting has gone through numerous changes, clients remain the same. They have egos, and it does not matter what industry you are talking about. No one industry or profession has a monopoly on egos. A consultant will find them emerging regardless of the profession. "Handle with care" is a good motto to follow.

The ego factor is only one element consultants have to be wary of when dealing with clients. There are others. Jack Branberg says some consultants run afoul of the client because they do "process consulting." That is, they follow certain steps, no matter what the project or relationship. They act in a specific manner, and do not adjust for the situation. Adler is an example of a consultant following a process. For years, he handled clients in a specific manner, designing communication programs based on his previous experience.

THE PROCESS PROBLEM

Process consulting is a hangover from the 1980s. Practitioners used the cookie cutter approach. If it worked well with one client, it should work well with others. Treat all clients the same, and develop programs and solutions through a specific process instead of customizing a program based on a client's needs.

In the 1980s, process consulting worked well because a good percentage of solutions developed by consultants never got out of the CEO's office. Implementation never took place, thus no one knew that there was a weakness in the process. Today, however, decision makers want the consultants to implement their solutions. The process approach will not work. Each job takes individual analysis and customized planning. One shoe will not fit all.

There are consultants who are still using the process method. They develop proposals and solutions in the same manner for every client. They have set questions they ask of clients, and rarely do they deviate from them. This approach is not highly successful. With the mammoth corporate changes that have gone on during the past few years, problems within companies differ greatly.

For example, morale problems, which, in the past, were usually attributed to ineffective supervisors, are looked at differently today. They may be caused by everything from poor supervisors to a shortage of workers. To find out which is the culprit, the consultant has to delve into the company, ask questions, and find out what is happening. Coming in with a page full of mimeographed questions, does not cut it anymore.

Consultants who utilize process consulting exclusively usually do not get the business, or they lose the account quickly. Consultants have to listen well to avoid falling into the process trap.

THE DISTANCE GAP

Dealing with clients in the 1990s has its advantages and disadvantages. In the 1980s, if you were 100 miles away, a client would have qualms about hiring you. Today, you can be 3,000 miles away, and clients do not think twice about giving you the account—if they believe you can do the job. At the same time, the decision makers expect you to have a firm grasp on their company and the project. They want consultants to understand that their company is unique, and it requires innovative solutions. Not the same exact answers that have been given to 100 other companies through the same process. It is chemistry more than geography that binds the relationship between the consultant and the client.

To ensure that there is chemistry, an important ingredient in any client/consultant arrangement is communication. "Frequent communication," says Branberg, "is critical. Talk to them [the client] when you are at the company and tell them the bad as well as the good. Especially the bad. Sooner or later that comes out, and if you have been hiding it the relationship will suffer."

Importance of Status Reports

Regardless of how good the relationship happens to be, Branberg and others do weekly status reports, especially on larger projects. The report can be written or verbal, depending on whether or not the consultant is on-site. The length of the report is not critical, rather "it is the frequency that counts," cautions Branberg.

Who gets the report? It should be the person who does the hiring, unless otherwise specified by the company. At the very least, the person who did the hiring should be copied on reports. Consultants should use judgment here, too. When you are hired, how many executives were in the meeting? Are they all involved? Should they all be kept informed?

Initial meetings are ideal for determining who should get communiques once the project is underway. The consultant's ability to "read" people enters into this phase. Who is asking the questions? Who is making the decisions? At times, it may be the same person, but often it is not.

Not every client understands what a consultant does, or is supposed to do. The 10 practitioners in this book deal in diverse, complex fields. Their challenge is not only to solve the problem but, at the same time, help the client understand what is going on. Clients know their business. They do not know consulting, or what goes into it. The more you can explain and report, the healthier the relationship.

Andrea Needham says in her field some clients are confused, and have a difficult time deciding what they want. They just want the problem solved, but there are no easy solutions. "You have to convince management of that." Sometimes, management is looking for the "magic bullet." They may have heard about some phenomenal new technique or method that solves everything. When the consultant arrives they ask for the "pill." Mike Green puts some of the quality programs that have attained a high degree of popularity in this category.

"TQM (Total Quality Management) is a gimmick," he says. "It is something that makes management and employees feel warm and happy. It has helped a great many management consultants sell books and generate business, but if someone begins to talk about the importance of TQM to their company, be careful. They could turn out to be a difficult client."

Laurie Mirman says every industry has its quirks and habits. In hers, a new consultant may negotiate a rate with a hotel on behalf of the client, and suddenly find that the standard rate was raised in anticipation of the negotiation. The consultant proudly tells the client the new, "lower" rate and ends up looking foolish.

Impact of Change

"You may feel you have just negotiated your client a tremendous savings on a block of rooms, only to find the hotel was 'waiting' for you. They raised the $100 rate to $125 and then let you 'negotiate' it to

$95. After you have been in this business, you get used to some of the things people do. But, just when you think you know what to expect, something new pops up. This is a changing business, and you have to stay on top of it. I think the same is true of every consulting field. Things change."

They do. Remember, in just a few years, consulting has gone through major changes. Retainers are out, projects are in; networking is gone and relationship marketing has arrived; the high rise is out, and the home office is in. Individual professions have seen just as much change, and that impacts the way you deal with clients—and the way they deal with consultants.

Rudy Dew's outplacement company is a good example. He has been in the field for a decade and in the beginning outplacement was a service provided primarily to executives. Companies paid for programs, and laid off senior managers were the prime beneficiaries. But, industry has changed. Executives have been joined by middle-managers, and middle-managers have been joined by others in the work force. Layoffs and cutbacks are nondiscriminatory. Everyone is subject to them, and Dew has altered his practice according to the client's changed needs.

Although he still does major outplacement business with companies that utilize his services for executives, he also has outplacement programs for those at the security guard level. His company even offers outplacement in Spanish.

Dew not only added services to meet the changing needs of his clients, but he anticipated them. Successful consultants do the same. How? They read, watch, and ask questions. Cindy Novotny never used to read, however, today she never misses an issue of *The Wall Street Journal* or a host of other business publications. "Remember, you need to know what's going on, and how it will impact your business. I read because I'm afraid I am going to miss some new development; some new technique that perhaps we should be using."

DEALING WITH COMPETITION

Being aware means more than knowing what new innovations are hitting your industry. It also means an awareness of competitors.

Who is competing for the project? What approach will they take? How will they try and sell the client? What can you do to make a better impression?

In the final analysis, a consultant is successful in selling their services because they left a lasting, positive impression or had better rapport than the competition. Vying with other companies for business, is no different than going out for a job interview. The candidate with the best rapport is usually going to be the one that is hired.

Branberg recalls one project he was awarded while competing against one of the Big Six consulting firms. He had done a half-dozen projects for the client and was invited to make a presentation. The Big Six firm was, too. But, Branberg did not take anything for granted. He knew what the project entailed and had contacted several members of his consortium; people who would be working on the project. Instead of visiting the company by himself and making the presentation, he took along the other experienced professionals who knew about the project.

The Big Six firm came in with senior partners. Heavyweights, but not the consultants who would be doing the work. The partners were the salespeople. The Big Six team spent about an hour with the client, outlining their skills, and so on. Branberg's team came in and spent more than three hours—discussing the firm's problems. Branberg got the project.

RELATIONSHIP ADVANTAGE

An advantage to bringing the people in who will work on the account is that the consultant has an opportunity to establish rapport with the client and the people who will be doing the work. The consultant can show that his or her consulting team can work with the company's internal people. If the team gets along and has rapport with the decision makers, it can get along with the employees when it comes time for implementation. That is the impression that is left. A team of salespeople, who are only there to close the deal, do not leave the same impression.

"You can be the smartest consultant in the world," says Branberg, "but if you cannot work with people, you are not going to make it in this business. I bring my team so that the client can see we are real people, just like his employees. And, we can work with his employees, too.

"If you cannot work with the company's people, all the brilliant ideas in the world will not matter. They will never be implemented, and that is not where consulting is today. CEOs do not hire firms for solutions. They hire them to develop solutions, and to work with employees to implement them." Management regard their employees as a valuable asset. They want them to feel involved. To be part of the decision-making and implementation process.

Initial client meetings are crucial to the relationship. They are critical gatherings where management decides who is going to get the project. But, they are sounding boards, too. Consultants use them to find out what the client thinks and how they regard the practitioners who are making the presentation. Within a half-hour, a consultant can tell if there is going to be rapport. If there is not, and the consultant takes the project, trouble is virtually guaranteed.

CONSULTANTS NEED INNOVATIVE SOLUTIONS

Consultants are called in to find a new way to solve problems. Corporations have—and are—changing dramatically. Some of the changes are best illustrated by looking at two related consulting professions—organization and compensation. In the "old" (1980s) days, compensation was usually based on the shape of the organization chart. It was a typical pyramid, and the executive who had more "boxes" reporting to him usually was the highest paid.

Today, the organization chart is having problems. Needham thinks it is on the way out. "Clients want people to work together in teams," says Needham. "Teams do not work in layers, like the layers of a chart. You have to tip the chart on its side, and you get a better picture of what the organization should look like. Not everyone on the team may get the same base pay, but to have effective teams the bonus compensation should be similar for everyone on the team."

Those are major changes for management to accept, and they are only a few of the reasons why consulting is a challenge. "We not only have to come up with the solutions, but often we have to fight tradition.

CEOs have a difficult time accepting changes to their traditions," says Needham.

KNOW THE DECISION MAKERS

CEOs are not always the people making the decisions. Consultants find employees have power. With staff reductions, companies have held onto the best employees. However, the cutbacks have left employees cynical. They have seen good, highly qualified, long-term peers laidoff. They know they may be next. At the same time, the company values these remaining individuals. They are highly skilled and would be difficult to replace. They are the best of the best.

Decision making may remain with the CEO, but a wise chief executive is not going to pull against his employees. He is going to choose a program—and consultant—that not only gets along well with executives, but with the other employees as well. In some cases, it is not unusual for the decision makers to bring in several of the lower echelon managers to determine how they feel about the consultant. Do they like him or her? Do they think the consultant can work with other employees?

A decade ago, it did not matter if the employees liked the consultant or not. In many cases, employees disliked consultants. They saw them as threats, people who were coming in to evaluate how poorly the employee did his or her job; people who were going to make recommendations to management on how to save money by reducing the number of employees. There was jealousy and anxiety. For the most part, it was a negative experience.

Compounding the consulting/employee relationship was the fact many practitioners came in and were built up as people who knew all the answers. If they did not know, they could find them. Successful consultants do not display that attitude today.

"I tell them," says Branberg, "I do not know all the answers. That's true. I tell them I do not know the company as well as they do, and I will need their help." With the new downsized structure of most companies, consultants are more likely to be welcomed by employees. They are seen as professionals who can help, instead of efficiency experts who are there to measure performance or suggest where to cut staff.

Not all employees welcome consultants with open arms. Green says these employees, instead of being a hindrance, can help. "The consultant needs someone within the company who will not readily accept all his ideas. He needs a sounding board, some opposition. I need 'rafter rattlers' because they often have the best ideas, or they are excellent evaluators of your ideas."

To Green, the consultant should not be searching for the perfect world. Accept those with different opinions and get the most out of them; find out why their opinions are so removed from your own. "You never know," he says, "they may know something that even senior management is not aware of."

HANDLING EMPLOYEES

Today, a group of employees complaining about a consultant can cost the practitioner a project. Management prefers to tread lightly. Employees have gone through stressful times. They expect consultants to build rapport with people throughout the company, and not just with the senior executives.

Brad Leggett has not lost sight of this influence. He stresses to workers within client companies that he is on the job to help them; to make their job easier. His success depends greatly on "how they perceive me. Do they see me as a help or are they concerned about what my report may say about them. Rapport alleviates those concerns, regardless of what consulting field you are in."

Branberg says "this is a people business. Aside from excellent communication skills, the consultant has to have superior people skills."

"A consultant," explains Branberg, "is unlike the typical salesperson. They do not just market a traditional product and leave the rest to the 'service' department. Consulting takes time . . . it takes building."

RETAINER VERSUS PROJECTS

Once a consultant has passed muster by the senior managers and the company's employees, hiring can be in one of several forms. First, there is the retainer. Clients are hesitant to offer this type arrangement. In the 1980s, agreements almost always involved retainers, and many companies found they spent funds needlessly. They did not need a consultant around continuously. The retainer usually meant the consultant was not there for a specific need.

Today, clients prefer the project basis. CEOs and other decision makers are reluctant to commit funds on an ongoing basis. They do not want to sign three-, six-, or nine-month or even year-long agreements. They are nervous about spending too much or hiring someone who will end up standing around for half the term of the agreement. There is also a problem that many decision makers have of not completely understanding what a consultant does. Who is going to monitor the consultant and the team? Who is going to determine if they are doing things right? With a project and clearly defined goals, decision makers can track progress and see results more clearly.

For almost every professional, it is a project business. If you do the project well enough, it could work into a retainer. That happens when the client gets to know the practitioner extremely well, respects their opinion, and wants their ideas on other projects. "When you build that strong a relationship," explains Branberg, "you can begin to look for the retainer. That takes a great performance on projects as well as relationship building."

Stern says many decision makers use consultants as they would a "temporary agency." There is minimum commitment of funds. "Don't forget," he says, "many companies prefer a project or temporary arrangement because they have been burned before."

SOME BUSINESS IS NOT GOOD BUSINESS

When you are paying the bills, consultants are tempted to take any and every project that comes along. It is a natural reaction. But, Beekman says the consultant should be asking questions before they take an account. Do you believe in this client and what they want to do? Is it possible? Do you want to work with them? Invariably, the consultant who tries to shortcut and take a project merely for the fee is going to strike out and cause hard feelings as well as get a bad reputation by word-of-mouth.

Beekman asks other questions, "Will this account add to my client mix?" For example, could the account be a conflict with another similar product and/or service company? Beekman believes that consultants should diversify and work in more than one industry. Aside from the consultant enlarging his or her sphere of relationships, working in a variety of industries is a form of job security. If one industry falters, the consultant can always pick up the slack by increasing efforts in one of the other areas in which he or she has been working. Novotny has made diversification a critical part of her practice.

NEW ROLE FOR PART-TIMERS

The bane of all consultants and the person who does the most damage to the profession is the part-timer. Part-timers usually fall into several categories. There is the executive who has the skills, but not necessarily the consulting expertise. Just because someone is familiar with an industry does not mean they can provide counseling to a firm. Nor does it mean they can deal with clients.

Some part-timers are in consulting because they are testing the waters. If things work, and they are able to get clients, they will go into it full-time. But, a half-commitment never makes for good business. Nor does it make for good relationships with clients.

A decade ago, there was room for part-timers. Demands differed as did the clients. The business has changed. There are a multitude of horror stories about part-time consultants. Most revolve around laid-off executives who were merely hanging out their shingle because they were between jobs. They were usually more concerned with finding a job, then developing solutions for the client's problem. Some of these between-job executives are super salespeople, and they generated clients. They also gave the profession a bad name. Before the company realizes it, but after the consultant has collected fees, he regretfully resigns the project because he has found a fulltime position with a company.

Although there are mixed feelings among some consultants, the majority say there is no way a practitioner can work themselves into a full-time enterprise from a part-time beginning. Most of these 10 consulting professions do not lend themselves to part-time work.

Dan Potter points out one simple difficulty that someone would have if they worked a full-time job and tried to start a part-time consulting profession. "Clients want to see the consultant during working hours, 9 to 5 P.M. That means the consultant cannot be working full-time elsewhere. It does not work, at least not when it comes to executive search."

Green agrees, "None of the jobs I have done during the past two years, could be done by a part-timer. The demands of the client are too great. They do not want to see you at 6:30 in the evening or 6:30 in the morning." Many CEOs or decision makers who have been burned by part-timers or inadequately skilled practitioners view consulting with suspicion for another reason—they do not understand it. There are few clients who really comprehend the consultant and what they do. A consultant may be representing a high-tech client with new software. The client's expertise is in producing software, the consultant's in marketing and positioning the product.

It is the same syndrome that impacts other professions. For example, most businesspeople know that advertising should bring in business, but they are not sure how the process works. Why do you advertise in one publication and not another? Why do you place an ad in the main news section instead of the business page?

Look at public relations (PR). Clients understand the professional PR person can enhance their image by getting positive stories in print, but how does the public relation's practitioner get the material in print? What's the process?

For that matter, you can take almost any professional, and when they come together with another area of expertise, they may have heard about it, but they do not understand how it works. And, when we do not understand things, we tend to mistrust them.

In other ways, a client's inability to understand what a consultant does is beneficial. Consultants prefer having some mystique about the way they operate. If there was not any, and the client understood completely, he or she would soon begin to wonder "why am I paying for something that I can do myself?" That isn't a healthy attitude (from the consultant's perspective) for any client to have.

The consultant who inadvertently says "I can solve that in a snap" is not impressing a client. Instead, they are endangering their relationship with the client, and probably heading down the road to losing the account. Why? With "snap" statements you leave the impression that perhaps this job was not too difficult after all . . . perhaps we did not need a consultant . . . perhaps we wasted our money. The wise consultant understands this and *never* indicates *any* job will be easy.

Successful client relationships depend a great deal upon the consultant being viewed as an expert; someone who can offer something to the project that no one else can. Remove that image, and the question quickly emerges as to whether "we should have spent the money."

Dew ran into one that was easy, but had all the earmarks of a difficult problem. He was called in by a CEO who was frustrated with a senior manager that the CEO always imagined to be a good employee.

Dew asked what the problem was, and the CEO told him that one of his key executives had suddenly started coming in late every morning. While everyone else arrived at 6–7 A.M., this executive arrived at 9 A.M.

The CEO could not understand it, but he wanted Dew to handle the situation. He was about to fire the manager, and was thinking of using Dew's firm for outplacement services. "Something did not seem right," recalls Dew. "Why would an executive with an exemplary record suddenly turn sour?"

Dew asked the CEO for details. The president explained that "I get in at 6 A.M., and every morning about 9 A.M. I look out at the lot and he is the last person pulling in. We need to get rid of him."

Before making any hasty decisions, Dew decided to watch the lot for a few days and talk to the executive. Dew met with the executive and asked if there was a reason he was the last person in the lot? That's when the senior vice president explained that he had just purchased a new car, and did not want to get it scratched. To avoid nicks and scratches, when he arrived—at 6 to 6:30 A.M.—he parked in the back of the lot, where no one else had their car. About 9 A.M. he would come out and move his car into the executive spaces.

Simple problem, easily solved? The case illustrates how the consulting process should be conducted. Dew could have suggested that the CEO ask the executive why he was late, but that would not have sufficed. The CEO called Dew because he perceived a problem; a problem that went much deeper than asking a question. Perhaps the executive was thinking of leaving? Maybe he had another offer from a rival firm? Would he be taking trade secrets?

Would it have been resolved more rapidly if Dew had suggested that the CEO simply ask the executive why he was late? Of course, however, that is not the consultant's job. Dew's task was to first listen to the client, understand the problem/need and then come up with a method to solve it.

Every consultant has the same task when they work for a client. Asking the executive why he was late might have answered the CEO's question quickly, but it could have led to misunderstandings. Suppose the executive was visiting another firm; a rival? If that were the case, Dew might never have uncovered the true reason for the tardiness.

THE NEED FOR LISTENING, ANALYTICAL SKILLS

This case illustrates how important strong listening and analytical skills are to a consultant. The consultant has to read between the lines; to listen to a CEO and not take everything literally. Clients frequently perceive things differently, and only the perceptive, questioning practitioner is able to find the truth.

Consultants have to be willing to take risks, too. Needham says every practitioner is a risk taker. "Once you recommend a solution and stand behind it, there is always a risk; the chance you are wrong."

One of the most misunderstood consulting professions is communication/public relations. Clients understand the value of good publicity, but have trouble comprehending how the media gets its material, and how the consultant generates coverage. Clients also have difficulty understanding why the media sometimes prints things that are inaccurate. They also wonder why it is so difficult to get a retraction, when there is an error.

When a client retains someone like Beekman, and they see their name and comments in print, it suddenly occurs to many that what they said does not always look the same in print.

There is an "understanding gap" between client and consultant and there will always be one. If the client understood too much, they might not be willing to pay the tab. If we understood exactly how a brain surgeon operates, part of the mystique would be removed and, perhaps, we would be wondering why they get paid more than other professionals.

Mystique counts. Practitioners should never simplify their profession to the point the client understands it as well as his or her own. If they do, that question will invariably pop up—"Is this consultant really worth that much?"

THE BIG "I" CHANGE

One of the major changes the consultant finds in the 1990s is what Branberg calls the "Big I"—Implementation. Decision makers do not just want a 30-page proposal with suggestions. They want a solution, and they want it implemented. And, consultants want to be involved.

A decade ago, the consultant was faced with the problem of delving in, researching, finding the problem, developing a solution, and turning it over to management for implementation. These expensive reports sat on bookshelves or in back rooms, and nothing was ever done with them. They became a source of frustration for both the consultant and management.

The desire for the Big "I" has changed all that. "The client," says Branberg, "should not be paying the consultant to write huge procedure manuals. We want to participate. We should be involved. Every consultant should."

Involvement helps the consultant build a reputation and trust with the client. It forces the consultant to come up with practical solutions. Practicality was not a concern in the 1980s, because the consultants rarely had to see their solutions through to fruition.

JUDGING CONSULTING PERFORMANCES

Aside from implementation, there are usually two ways a consultant can judge how well the job was done, and what the client thought of them. "Did the client offer you a job," smiles Branberg, "or did he offer you another project?" A "yes" to either one of those questions tells you how you did. "That's really the best critique of your performance."

The job offer rarely comes before implementation. The Big "I" is done in several possible ways. The consultant may work directly with the senior managers and a team of employees, or they can be utilized to be the project managers, while the employees implement the solution.

As a rule, consultants do not try to implement without the cooperation of employees. When an outsider does something without the assistance of those within the company, it never works or sticks. Companies respect that attitude, and rather than create resentment it usually improves rapport and builds relationships between management and the consultant.

Gerry Stern says that everything the consultant does is geared toward building those relationships. From the initial contact with a client, to the proposal and the implementation. Even after the project is done, an astute consultant will maintain relationships with key people at the firm.

SUMMARY

The challenge the consultant faces is not only generating business and solving problems, but "adding value" to the client's business as well. That's what CEOs want. They do not want to hire an expensive practitioner and have them turn in solutions that do not improve the company's sales or service.

In the 1990s and beyond, the phrase that consultants must remember when dealing with clients is "adding value." To help clients improve performance, and the bottom line. That is the ultimate goal and motivator of every CEO, and it should be the goal of consultants, too.

CHAPTER 5

WRITING PROPOSALS, SETTING FEES, AND BILLING

This story is well-known among marketing consultants. It took place in a small city, and involved a nonprofit organization and the marketing practitioner the group was interviewing. The nonprofit was struggling to raise funds, and it decided to bring in a professional, who could give them ideas as to how they might increase the donations they received. They began by interviewing several marketing consultants, and eventually decided on one, a bright, young practitioner who had just opened his doors.

His openness and willingness to share ideas impressed them. The offer he made could not be beat. He proposed examining the nonprofit's marketing program, detailing the problems that he saw, and offering solutions. No cost, no obligation. The board readily agreed, and told him if his proposal met their expectations, the job was his.

The consultant spent weeks at the nonprofit, interviewing employees, and people who donated funds. During the research process, he discovered some of the objections donors had and what it would take to overcome those feelings.

Anxiously, the consultant went back to his office and prepared a lengthy, in-depth proposal. It covered everything. It detailed the problems, why they existed and what could be done to alleviate them. The consultant even recommended a path of action, and showed how additional funds could be raised.

He called the board, made an appointment, and a week later found himself before the 12-member group, making his presentation. He spent more than two hours detailing his findings and recommendations. The board loved it, and told him so. As he left, they told him he would hear from them within the next 48 hours.

Time passed and nothing happened. A week later, the consultant was no longer able to contain himself. He called the nonprofit's director. The call was never returned. Ten days later, he received a curt note from the board. It thanked him for his interest, however, after much discussion, the board had decided they could not afford the program he recommended. They were cognizant of the work he put into the project, but they had decided not to retain an outside consultant at this time.

The practitioner was shattered. Disappointed, he finally was able to forget his effort and concentrate on new prospects. Within a few months, he had almost forgotten his ill-fated effort. That is, until one day he opened the newspaper and saw it. There was a full-page advertisement for the nonprofit. Only this ad was different from the ones the organization normally ran. This one carried a new headline and different copy. It was the theme and copy the consultant had detailed in his proposal months before.

Ten years ago—when that happened—a consultant had to be a "creative manipulator" when writing a proposal. The practitioner had to show the client that they had an excellent understanding of the situation, and a clear idea on how to solve the problem(s).

One of the few ways to demonstrate that expertise, was to write a proposal detailing the problem and then offering solutions. Unfortunately, some consultants—like the one who wrote the proposal for the nonprofit—got carried away with the solution portion, and not only outlined ideas but detailed them, too. As a result, many prospective clients took the proposal and ran with it.

Within a short time, consultants had found ways to put a positive spin on their proposals without revealing everything. The young marketing consultant in this case became a pro at it. A year after he had faced the nonprofit board, he found himself in front of a large real estate conglomerate. The company was about to build a multimillion-dollar, five-year project, and it was looking for outside marketing assistance. This time, the creative consultant came up with ideas, but did not spell out the implementation steps. A day after he presented it, the real estate firm's CEO called him and gave him the project.

As is the case with many consultants, the marketing practitioner learned that in presentations it was best to avoid specifics. Stick to generalizations. If there is a solution, do not detail how you are going to get to it.

PROTECTING PROPOSAL IDEAS

Stealing ideas and milking the consultant for knowledge and free advice, has always been a problem. One that consultants will never escape. Most clients can be trusted but there are always a few who are willing to take the solutions, thank the consultant, say goodbye, give it to their internal staff, and run.

There was more stealing and brain picking in the 1980s. Today, most clients have a problem if they take a proposal and run—there are not enough knowledgeable employees remaining to carry out the plan. With downsizing, the relationship between consultant and client added a new dimension. Clients were not just calling consultants for ideas, but to develop and implement them as well.

NEW TYPE PROPOSAL

Proposals have become more open and detailed. This openness is not just due to a cutback in employees. Much of it has been made possible because of the new relationship that has developed between many consultants and the prospect.

The proposal has also taken on a new dual role. Typically, a proposal outlines the consultant's qualifications, the problems the practitioner perceives, and the solutions. Today's proposals include all this plus they also outline what the consultant will do, when it will be done, and how much it will cost. It is a more thorough, detailed document. It has become an agreement and reminder. Because of the additional role, proposals—which were once an exercise in generalization—are now concrete and specific, and have become an important part of the consultant's presentation.

Nearly every consultant emphasizes how important proposals are, and the critical role a proposal plays not only in selling the client, but in helping to make a fuzzy profession (consulting) more understandable.

Carol Beekman says that the proposal "initially is a document that outlines everything we are going to do for the client. It has billing procedure, payment, terms and so on. The client signs it and we each retain a copy." It is a contract.

One of the values of the proposal is that clients may not understand exactly how the job will be done, but they have "a clear view of what will be done," says Beekman.

Jack Branberg insists that every client get a proposal. It not only clarifies the job, but makes the "client think." The client sees, in black-and-white, exactly what will be done and when. Branberg says every consultant should utilize one.

The proposal serves two other important purposes. It is a measurement or benchmark tool. At any time, the client can pull it out and see how much of the project the consultant has finished, and how close they are to the timetable. It protects the client, and enables them to question the consultant with something concrete in hand.

It protects the consultant, too. At times, clients forget exactly what the project entails. Once a consultant goes to work, other problems may surface. Naturally, the client wants the consultant to solve these problems, too, however, the practitioner has not included them in the bid. By utilizing the written proposal, and pointing out the items that are included, the consultant refreshes the client's mind as to what was expected. If additional services are needed, by examining the proposal the client can see that they must budget extra monies for it. The proposal is a check system for both the client and consultant. Everyone benefits. It keeps misunderstandings from developing.

Proposals keep both practitioners and client on course. Branberg says that sometimes the consultant works hard and is going one way, but the client expects him to go another. With a proposal "that does not happen. The client understands and can correct us, and it is our insurance policy, too."

The Executive Summary

Beekman—as do other consultants—utilizes the proposal as a formal plan. It opens with an executive summary—an overview of the situation and how the consultant is going to deal with the problem. A prospect can read the summary, which usually runs less than a page, and get the gist of the entire proposal.

Handshake versus Proposal

Mike Green, one of the few consultants who tries to avoid proposals, nevertheless agrees that a comprehensive document helps prevent misunderstandings between clients and consultants. He prefers a handshake, but with some clients, that is not possible. Several of his projects involve clients who have government contracts, and the bureaucratic process requires a detailed outline (proposal) of what the consultant is going to do. Cindy Novotny does proposals for every client. They usually run about four to five pages, and they detail every aspect of the sales training she is going to conduct.

Most consultants view the proposal as a positive part of the consulting process, but Stern cautions that there can be a drawback. "Don't write a proposal and drop it off," he says. "Especially if you are competing for the project. Proposals take explanation, selling. Every one of them should be accompanied by a verbal presentation, and consultants should get the prospect to agree to one."

A proposal in Dan Potter's case is a must. Potter's proposal is a menu of services, and gives the client a variety of choices. They can pick and choose anything from $5,000 to $15,000. The menu driven proposal has proven to be the thing that differentiates Potter's firm from all others in the executive search field. It has been such a hit, that Potter credits much of his rapid growth to it. It could be applicable in other consulting areas, too.

Potter has constructed his cafeteria menu with the customer in mind. Depending upon what the client wants, that's how much the fee will go up and down. It is a creative approach to a traditional document, and it is one of the things that has made him such a success in the 18 months he has been in business. Similar applications are possible in other consulting fields. Potter explains he has "unbundled" the executive search process, and by separating the elements and pricing them differently, his proposal has become an excellent sales tool.

His most inexpensive proposal offers the client numerous time-saving search benefits. But, it does not involve Potter in every aspect of the search. For instance, the interviewing is still done by the company. The most expensive proposal involves Potter in the search from beginning to the end (hiring).

Potter's proposals are written to show clients how much can be saved in search dollars as well as employee time. The client does not have to use a human resource director or clerical help to write copy, place ads, cull resumes, or interview candidates. The proposal drives that point home. Potter usually presents a verbal addition, which points out that the cost of one ad in a major market can easily be greater than his fee for the entire project. Rarely does Potter lose a prospective client once they have seen and heard his unbundled approach.

RESEARCH FOR PROPOSALS

Regardless of a proposal's format, they take time to put together. It takes Brad Leggett two or three trips to a client's company before he can gather enough data to construct one. Each visit can run to two hours. Leggett does not mind putting in the time. He views proposals as one of the most important selling tools in the consultant's arsenal. He takes his time and feels "it is a mistake to put one together hurriedly."

In writing the proposal, Leggett advises other consultants to make sure they understand what the client wants, not what "you think they should get." Focus on the client's needs and "understand how to get the results that will meet those needs." Leggett uses a two-step process in constructing a proposal. He does his initial research and interviews, and returns with a draft proposal. He asks the decision makers to examine and critique it. At this point, revisions, if any, are noted.

The draft proposal is becoming commonplace. Consultants usually outline what they will do (with proposals) to clients upfront. They let them know a draft will be written first. The time investment for putting together a first-class, detailed proposal is such that most consultants want to have guidance from the client before they finalize the document. Thus, the draft and a visit to the client give them input.

If Leggett comes away from that meeting feeling that he has captured the project with the exception of minor additions or changes, he formalizes the draft, has it typed in final form, and returns with a proposal that concludes with a brief letter of agreement on the final page. Leggett and the client then sign it. If he has missed any points, he goes back to the research phase.

CHARGING FOR PROPOSALS

It would be nice to be compensated for the time it takes to prepare a proposal, however, consultants rarely ask for compensation for the proposal. There are exceptions. For instance, if the practitioner has been asked to prepare a proposal that analyzes the problem, solves it in detail, gives exact steps that the client should follow to implement the solution, there is usually a fee.

Today, research and proposal writing can take almost as long as the job itself, but aside from the previously mentioned situation, the consultant does not get a fee for writing one. It is part of the marketing process.

If the proposal is done correctly, the conversion rate from prospect to client "is excellent" says Leggett. Leggett usually closes half the prospects for whom he writes proposals.

THE TIME FACTOR

Stern and Branberg spend an enormous amount of time researching and putting the proposal together. Stern will take 10 hours or more talking to workers on an assembly line if he is working on a reorganization plan. Branberg may spend more. As an example, Branberg described a typical case where he and an associate went out, met with the prospective client, and determined the needs. They came back again for clarification of several points, and before they were done, they had spend in excess of six hours interviewing the senior manager and his staff.

Branberg then put together a draft proposal and submitted it. He says that first proposal—which comes with no cost or obligation—is critical in determining if he is on-target. Afterwards, he returned with a revised, final version, and presented it orally to the decision makers. Once again, at no cost.

The care and time that all consultants put into proposals is evidence of how important the process has become. A well-crafted document shows the prospect that you have grasped the situation and understand the company.

Branberg also does a creative "semi-formal" proposal. He will visit a past or prospective client, and feed him ideas that are presented in a structured format, similar to a proposal. When he presents good ideas, they usually result in projects coming his way. To operate in this manner, a consultant has to have an excellent relationship with the prospect. Usually, it is someone that Branberg has done business with previously.

Consulting is a competitive business, and if a prospect runs into a practitioner who wants to be paid to prepare a proposal, he can always find another consultant—equally as competent—who will not charge.

NO FEE DISCOUNTS

Clients expect free proposals, but they do not look for discounts and freebees when it comes to fees. Companies know the value of consulting services, because of the employees who once performed the same function.

Clients do not want something for nothing. In the 1980s, consultants frequently supplied valuable information and got nowhere. It was often brainpicking time. Now, the insight and information more often leads to a project and contract. When the consultant is hired, the fees are paid without any qualms.

Consultants also run into prospective clients who have a specific budget in mind. If the budget makes economical sense, the practitioner does not have a problem. But, what if it does not? What happens if the company has been unrealistic? What can the consultant do?

Do not tackle the project if you are going to lose money. Occasionally, if the client is new and the consultant believes that the prospect may provide additional business, he or she might take project on a breakeven basis. However, accepting one where there is a loss is a mistake. It never works out. The consultant begins to feel cheated and starts ignoring the project in favor of another, better paying one. It's a natural reaction. Consequently, the client becomes unhappy, the relationship breaks down, and the consultant not only loses money and the client, but often the former client goes on to demean the consultant's reputation.

ESTABLISHING FEES

One factor behind the success of competent consultants is the great care they took in arriving at fees. Fee structures are changing. Companies are becoming more cost conscious, and although clients seldom quarrel over price, they want rationale. Why does it cost $X. Consultants should explain fees carefully. They detail the research that has to be done, the hours involved, and the expenses they will incur.

Surprisingly, fees have not escalated to any great extent. Hourly rates that were around in the 1980s are about the same today. Fee stabilization goes along with the emphasis companies have put on cost control. They do not want to pay more than is absolutely necessary.

Dan Potter's practice is a good example of price stabilization. Even though his service is unique, and saves clients time and money, he cannot raise his fees. He is being impacted by factors that apply not only to his industry (health care) but others, too.

CONSOLIDATION AND FEES

With health care, as is the case with many industries, consolidation is taking place. Big and small hospitals and facilities are merging. This has cut down the requirement for the number of projects given to search firms.

With fewer projects, those in the health care industry know they can negotiate with search firms and get a better deal. Negotiation is the rule when it comes to the contingency search firms that Potter competes against. Their overhead has remained high, but the number of projects have shrunk. Many are willing to take lower fees in order to "pay the rent" and make a smaller profit.

These firms charge anywhere from 30 percent to 35 percent of the executive's yearly salary, perks, and benefits. If a hospital administrator earns $100,000, the contingency company is going to ask for $30,000 to $35,000 to find the person to fill the position. Because of consolidation, the percentage has been driven down. Some large contingency firms will accept a search and charge as little as 20 percent.

Where does this put Potter? His prices are competitive (for instance, he will find a $100,000 executive for anywhere from $5,000 to $15,000), but he feels prices will drop. The contingency firms have to keep their doors open, and they will continue to lower their fees if pressed.

Examine Industry Fees

Potter's practice is an excellent gauge for others who are contemplating opening an office. Look at the fees that are prevalent in the business. Can you charge the same—or less—and still make a profit? Most consultants can, especially these 10 because of the demand for their services. Obviously, the greater the demand, the higher the price for the service.

Large Firm versus Small

Thanks to home offices, the disappearance of wining and dining, and the growing sophistication of clients, the viability (and profitability) of small consulting firms is greater than ever. In many instances, the one-person shop has not only been able to undercut the fees asked by the major firms, but show greater value to the client, too.

Clients know that the practitioner who works for a large firm and sells them on the service, may not be the consultant who does the work. A senior partner usually does the selling, and a junior or entry-level person does the work. This method, which is commonly practiced by most large firms, has helped Potter and others who are trying to compete against the majors.

Consultants use this as a selling point when they talk to prospective clients. It works. Imagine sitting across from a veteran consultant, and hearing that you will get his experience (20 plus years) and services, instead of a junior consultant with only a year or two in the field. Plus, the price of the veteran is usually going to be less.

The majors can match the expertise of any small consulting enterprise, but to remain economically viable, the larger organizations have to use their most knowledgeable people—those who are usually partners—as salespeople. Major firms tell the client, "Mary Jones will be working on the account with me, and if you have any question and I am not around, just ask for Mary."

Mary is capable of doing the work, but the client is constantly searching for the senior partner, the person who sold them. Relationships are rarely built by the senior partner or Mary. The partner is off selling while Mary is relegated to a support role. The client may never realize that Mary is doing the lion's share of the work.

THE SMALL CONSULTING FIRM ADVANTAGE

With the financial obstacles the large firms face, smaller consulting operations are making enormous competitive strides. Novotny, for instance, has little trouble with major competitors. "We are small and can get closer to the client. They do not have to crawl through corporate layers to see what we do and who is handling the training."

Branberg says the "prospects can sense the team (consortium) I put together is knowledgeable. We hit the ground running. That is no reflection on the ability of the young MBAs working for the majors, but they are at a disadvantage. They do not have the experience."

Branberg's teams are limitless in the expertise they have, and they satisfactorily answer the one prime question every client asks—can you solve my problem?

Stern has no employees, but he can walk in with more talent than any large consulting organization, thanks to his "virtual corporation." Andrea Needham has the same advantage. She not only utilizes her fellow consultants to help her complete the project, but she brings them in at the proposal stage as well.

DIFFERENCE IN FEES

While each of these 10 practitioners has a similar selling edge, they differ markedly from each other when it comes to fees. A few are paid by retainer, others earn their money based on the project, while some charge by the hour, or what the industry traditionally pays.

To determine how much (and how) to charge, each consultant in these 10 fields carefully surveyed the market to determine what competitors were charging. You cannot charge something outrageously high, regardless of how superior you believe your service to be. Today, clients rarely argue about price, but that does not mean there is not a sensitivity to costs. Today, clients watch costs closer than ever, and a consultant—regardless of the field—who is too high priced is not going to get the business.

Most of these practitioners started with fees that were slightly lower than their competitors. Most newcomers usually do the same. Potter's fees are lower than his contingency rivals. His menu-based services range from $5,000 to $15,000, whereas the contingency firm is going to be shooting for at least $20,000 in most of its searches. The contingency firm usually asks for one-third, which gives Potter a great deal of room to maneuver. Although Potter deals strictly in the health care field, the same fee structure will be found in other industries in which search consultants operate.

Hourly Charges

Needham has carefully examined the industry and the competition. Most compensation firms charge by the hour, anywhere from $300 to

$400. Needham's fees are lower and run about one-half ($150 to $200) the amount asked by the major consulting operations.

Beekman checked the competition and set her fees slightly lower than the person would at an agency (advertising and public relations). She also tacks on a small percentage for her experience. Agencies would classify her as a senior consultant, therefore her billable hours would be at the high end of the scale, although lower than an agency would charge if they supplied her services.

There are formulas that are used to arrive at fees, and they were used extensively in the 1980s. The most common is the "2,000 hour" approach. Consultants use 2,000 hours (per year) as a guide. This is the total number of hours it is possible to work when you take 52 weeks, subtract two for vacation, multiply the remaining 50 by 40 (hours per week), and you get 2,000.

From the 2,000, you subtract expenses (marketing, administration, bookkeeping, etc.) and you come up with a net number of hours. The consultant decides how much he wants to make a year, divides the net number of hours into it, and comes up with an hourly billing rate.

Take, for instance, a marketing consultant. If you use 2,000 hours as a yardstick, you would subtract marketing and administration activities. If one-third of a consultant's time is spent on marketing, the billable hours drop to 1,400. If billing and administrative work takes 200 more, the figure is down to 1,200. If the consultant wanted to make (gross) $150,000 a year, every billable hour would have to generate $125.00 per hour.

But, suppose marketing consultants are only earning (on the average) $100 an hour. The consultant could use the $125, but chances are he would not be signing many clients—unless he (or she) had a reputation and track record that were tops in the industry. The realistic goal is to price your services just under the top firms. Offer high quality service at a slightly lower cost. That's what enables most consulting practices to grow.

Another technique utilized is to determine your yearly costs, and then add on a desired profit. Include the salary in the costs. Next, determine how many working days there are in the year to earn that figure. Subtract weekends (104 days), desired vacations, holidays, possible sick days, and marketing time. (As a rule, you may spend up to one-third of every day in a marketing or business-building activity. This is especially true when you start out. The marketing time can go to 50 percent of every day.)

This scenario might be as follows:

Weekends	104 days
Vacation	10
Sick days	5
Holidays	7
Marketing	30

That adds up to a total of 156 days. Subtracted from 365, it leaves you 209 days. If your costs run $100,000 for salary, $20,000 for expenses and overhead, and you want to make an additional $25,000 in profit, you will have to earn $145,000 for 209 days. $209 \times 8 = 1,672$ hours divided into $145,000, equals about $87 an hour. You have to bill that for every working hour.

Realistically, what happens is the consultant bills what the market will bear. Hours and formulas are frequently tossed out. Green says his rates vary, depending upon the job and several other factors.

"If I have lots of work, I will charge a client more. If I have a lot of spare time, I'll drop my fee slightly."

HOW TIME IMPACTS BILLING

Green considers time frame, too. If a client wants it done "now," the consultant has to drop whatever they might be doing and devote time exclusively to the project. Urgency requires a higher fee, whether it be by the hour or on a project basis. Urgency keeps a consultant from handling a myriad of clients at the same time.

If a client wants something done in the next week, it might mean the consultant spends 100 percent of his time at the site. That keeps them from working elsewhere. Consequently, the urgent project costs the client more, because it prevents the practitioner from managing several projects at the same time and earning more money. When a project gets to the urgent classification, the client does not object to the higher fee. They just want the job done—quickly.

Green likes a project with "low demand time." That is, one that is not urgent. Low demand means he does not have to run to the site three times a week. If he has a four day consulting job, he will try and finish it in four weeks, which means one visit to the site/client each week. By spreading the time, the consultant also gets a better look at what's happening.

"If you are pushed to get something done fast," he says, "you may miss something. Projects that do not have the urgency factor become thorough jobs that make the client much happier. Look for them."

Stern's fee are under the major consulting companies, which charge anywhere from $300 to $400 an hour for reorganization. He bills about half that figure, and says he is highly competitive, because he is experienced, and a client could never get a knowledgeable reorganization practitioner for the rate he bills out.

Stern says that consultants must continually watch the market. "You get a good sense of what is being charged when you've been in the business for awhile. Nothing is cast in concrete. You hear through the grapevine . . . but there is no mechanical formula we use."

PERCENTAGE BASED FORMULA

There are formulas that are contemporary and intriguing. One of the boldest and most interesting is a concept that was developed in the sales and marketing arena. It is called "Percentage Plus." The consultant approaches the client, and proposes to take on the project if the client will compensate them based upon "increased sales."

For example, a client has a manufacturing concern and is planning to market a new product. The manufacturer estimates that the widget will generate an increase in sales of 10 percent for the first year. If the company normally sells $1 million worth of goods, and the new item is added, sales should be $1.1 million.

The practitioner takes the figure and agrees to take the project on without compensation. However, for every dollar over the projected $1.1 million in sales ($100,000 for the new item), the consultant gets 50 percent.

The consultant is crapshooting. They are saying we will take your item, develop a plan, market it, and put our best efforts forward and you do not have to pay us anything—unless we are successful. It is intriguing for the client, too. Imagine launching a new product line without allocating funds for marketing.

The plan has an obvious drawback. Suppose, the item is so much in demand that the market (consumers or whomever) want it regardless of the efforts put into the marketing plan? If that is the case, the client begins to resent paying a percentage of his sales. Or, suppose the consultant does a super job, and the item brings an additional $200,000, instead of $100,000 into the company. The consultant is going to collect $50,000—an amount that many manufacturers (or clients) may not be thrilled about giving. The approach is viable, and it can work with a client that does not have an abundance of capital.

SIMPLEST FEE-SETTING METHOD

The simplest method for fee-setting is to survey competitors, and decide how much under (or over) them you want to be. All it takes is calling one or two competitors, and indicating you might be in the market to utilize their services. Can they give you an idea of what it would cost? How do they work? Retainer? Hourly?

THE DEMISE OF RETAINERS

In the 1980s, retainers were commonplace. That is no longer the case. Most consultants work on a project basis, and the project has specific parameters spelled out. Sometimes, one project leads to another, such as Needham's executive compensation study opening the door for an hourly worker study.

Most consultants are flexible when it comes to fee setting. If the client prefers an hourly billing rate, they will provide it. If they want a project quote, they will design that.

In Beekman's case, a prospective client will say, here is the project, and they will ask her how long it will take, and what services will she provide. Beekman spells it out in a proposal, but gives an approximation of what the total project will cost. She will also do hourly billing, if the client prefers that.

To determine the hours a project will require takes experience. Branberg first estimates the amount of time (in person days) it will take to do the project. How does he figure the days? He spent more than 15 years with Peat Marwick and became an excellent judge of what a consultant could do in various time spans.

Some clients are not enamored with hourly billing because they feel it lends itself to overcharging. The consultant, for instance, spends 45 minutes and rounds it off to an hour. Beekman has overcome these objections by quoting a total fee at the beginning of the project.

Leggett uses both project and retainer, Green does it by project, and so does Branberg. Potter has based his entire marketing thrust on a menu service. Whether it is retainer, hourly, or project, there are several ways to bill. For projects, the billing may occur with one-third due when the contract/letter of agreement/proposal is signed, one-third in the middle of the project, and one-third at the conclusion.

Some consultants split the project into monthly billing or even less (every two weeks) if there are significant funds due. Another method is billing whenever "deliverables" are due. If the consultant has to prepare a special analysis, report, or whatever as part of the project, whenever one is due, the consultant bills a portion of the project.

Expenses are billed at the same time. When the monthly (or weekly) bill arrives, the expenses are listed. Receipts for any expenses are standard and important to the relationship. Some clients will pay expenses with or without the receipts, but it breeds mistrust if a tab is not there to back up the billing. Even small, seemingly insignificant expenses ($5 to $10) can irritate clients when the backup is missing.

HANDLING BILLINGS WITH ERRORS

There is a sensitivity to certain issues that revolve around billing. Backup for expenses is one, and miscalculation is another. For instance, what happens should the consultant err in calculating the cost of the project? Do they go back to the client and ask for more money? If so, how do they approach it?

Branberg has a definite policy. "If the increased expenditure is outside the scope of what we committed to do, I will go back to the client and explain it. I will go through the proposal and show them. I explain that we did not anticipate it, and we should explore it. On the other hand, if we committed to it as part of the project, and we simply misjudged what was involved, I will eat the additional expense."

Fees and what the client is going to get should be clearly spelled out in the final proposal. When a client questions the fees, Needham sits down and explains them. "But," she says, "I cannot remember the last time I had to go into details on the subject. Clients understand, if you spell it out in plain English."

IMPORTANCE OF WRITING

Fees and projects change, even after the client has signed and agreed to the terms. To avoid misunderstandings, the consultant reiterates conversations, points discussed, and any changes that may be desired by the client, in writing. A simple note saying, "I enjoyed meeting with you yesterday, and per our conversation, I will be doing . . . . XXX." That's all it takes, and the communication can save untold hours of grief.

When the client wants more than is in the proposal, Needham opens another project and calls it to the client's attention. "Do not let it go without saying something. If you fail to call it the client's attention, they will begin to think that it is part of the original proposal and project. They will continue to expect it."

THE CLIENT FEE RELATIONSHIP

The consultant, says Green, "also has to be able to read the client. That's the relationship marketing aspect. You have to be able to see between the lines. You might quote a fee, and they will never say it is 'too much.' They may hem and haw, but avoid the financial issue. They do not want to be embarrassed. If you cannot read this, you may miss the nuances of the conversation and never get the project. That's one of the reasons listening is a key skill."

Once the issue of fees is settled, an agreement is signed. Instead of lengthy, legal contracts, the most effective pact is one that is short and easy to understand. It can be a one-page letter or an addendum to the proposal. Leggett has a one-page letter, which protects him by spelling out when his fees are due. "It also protects the client. It tells them their rights to termination and the responsibilities that both of us have."

Branberg has the client sign the last page of the proposal, indicating they accept the project, what the objective of it is, the work plan, who is going to work on it, and the subcontractors (if any). "We put in the subcontractors so the client knows who we are utilizing and their expertise. Regardless of who they are, however, if anything goes wrong, we get the call."

USING SUBCONTRACTORS/FREELANCERS

Almost every independent consultant works with freelancers that they can call upon for assistance if a project is too big, or if it requires specialized expertise.

The freelancer is typically billed at his going rate plus a percentage. The percentage (markup) will range from 10 percent to 50 percent. If a freelancer gets $50 an hour, the client will be billed anywhere from $55 to $75, with the additional monies paying for overhead and bookkeeping.

Some freelancers get a piece of the action. Stern has run groups where there may be four or five consultants splitting a project, and they will split the revenue equally. Or, depending upon how much a freelancer has to do, they may get a smaller percentage.

Utilizing freelancers is a sophisticated part of the consulting industry. For the most part, they are talented, experienced professionals. Some might be retired CEOs, other might be senior executives who have been victims of downsizing. Still others may be consultants who own their own firms.

Branberg has his consortium of former CEOs, Stern his "virtual corporation," Potter has three researchers who will work on a project basis, Green has a list of fellow consultants who will all work on a project basis, Beekman has formed temporary partnerships, Leggett uses subcontractors, and so on. Every consultant can find help.

Subcontractors enable today's consultants to compete. The cross-section of subcontractors being utilized is interesting. Some would qualify as competitors, while a number bring added skills to the table that enhance the consultant's. When a consultant hires a subcontractor, part-timer or whatever, they should look for one with skills that complement their's—not abilities that are exactly the same. The broader the skills, the more impressive presentations are to clients.

Novotny says her subcontractors/associates all have different skills. One is an excellent salesperson, but does not want to get involved in the actual classroom training. He takes a part of the sales load off Novotny, so she can concentrate on providing the service.

She has an arrangement with another who enjoys training and selling, but does not want to work more than about 20 hours a week. She has a third who is an excellent classroom facilitator and trainer, but she does not have training programs at her disposal. Novotny supplies them and acts as a facilitator in her classroom as well. These relationships enable consultants to be more than one dimensional.

In the past, the consultant who was good at training, but poor at sales simply had to spend more time at sales. It could be frustrating. Or, they had to hire someone to do one aspect of the business. Today, that consultant works an agreement with a consultant who is good at sales.

These salespeople are similar to the representatives (reps) who have been around industries for years. A rep goes out and calls on retailers or distributors, and collects a commission of anywhere from about 6 percent to 15 percent.

Consultants have taken the same approach and hired reps, too. But, the reps who work for a consulting firm may be former consultants, or they may be professionals in the industry, who prefer sales to doing the actual work. They want to sign the client, and go onto the next one. They have no desire to get involved. Thanks to the reps, one person consulting firms have become efficient, and are able to compete with major consulting companies.

Beekman recently generated a client and project that was 2,000 miles away. She does a good portion of the work that was proposed, but she has another consultant she works with who is located in the same community as the client. He provides the liaison and communication between the firm (Beekman) and the client, while Beekman does most of the planning and execution of the communications plan.

Stern has taken subcontracting a step farther. Instead of just utilizing temporary help for a major project (or presentation), he belongs to a group of reorganization practitioners that meet regularly and discuss issues. They exchange ideas and brainstorm.

"The lone consultant," says Stern, "is no longer alone. It is possible to form groups like ours in every consulting profession. And, if they are competitors, all the better. They are used to dealing with the same issues, and you hear creative solutions."

Potter and others say you have to fit the "contract" consultants into the correct niche. Potter, for instance, uses them only for mundane portions of a project, such as compiling lists. If he uses them beyond name generation, he finds himself paying too large a portion of his retainer. "At that point, it does not make sense for me to be in business. Contract consultants can be an enormous help, but decide how you are going to use them, how much it is going to cost, and is it economical."

HOW MUCH DOES A CONSULTANT MAKE?

Once a consultant has paid the part-timers or contract consultants, and their overhead, what kind of income can they expect? The good ones—that is, those who operate like the 10 practitioners in this book—will generate six-figure incomes—for some, the gross profit is close to the $500,000 mark.

There are statistics that reveal what the average consultant makes, however, average does not apply to the 10 consultants we are discussing. Some consultants in reorganization make $250,000, while others, doing exactly the same thing and with the same skills, are in the $85,000 range. There is more to being profitable than doing the work. The same things that make the difference in the corporate world, impact a consultant's earnings. For instance, it takes discipline. The consultant has to get up every morning, market his services, and work for clients, too. The consultant has to be a skilled businessperson. They have to handle bookkeeping, and if they cannot do it, they must hire someone to assist them.

Rudy Dew, for instance, is an excellent consultant and businessperson. An outsourcing firm such as his will gross several million dollars in a typical year. "If you manage the business correctly," he says, "you will make anywhere from 9 percent to 30 percent in profit. But you have to be a good manager." While Dew is managing a healthy profit margin, there are several outplacement firms that have grossed more dollars than he did, but they lost money.

Consulting is a business. And it has to be run correctly. Consultants need as much accounting and marketing expertise as they do proficiency with their consulting skills. If they do not have those skills, they have to get someone on a part-time basis who does. Green, Novotny, Leggett, and Minar all run their businesses well and are extremely profitable. After 18 months, Potter's earnings have gone far beyond his projections.

Needham has a different philosophy when it comes to money and how much she makes. "I'm not sure," she says smiling. "To be honest, my guess is you should be working three to four days a week in my profession, and grossing about $1,600 a day. You should take four to six weeks off a year, bill three to four days a week for actual work— and live well."

Needham does. She likes "French champagne and I travel to New Zealand once a year. I enjoy myself and my business."

The same is true for every one of these winning consultants.

CHAPTER 6

THE GREAT PITFALLS

Regardless of the enormous potential for profitability that each of these 10 consulting fields have, there are pitfalls. In fact, not every practitioner has a successful business. Those who do not, have usually run into one or more of the following pitfalls.

1. Improper research
2. Oversell and underdeliver
3. Poor listening habits
4. Inadequate marketing
5. Building business, not relationships
6. Lack of business skills
7. Undercapitalization
8. Poorly written and executed proposals
9. Communication gap
10. Failure to explain the bills, expenses.

Every business has stumbling blocks, and despite the enormous opportunity in consulting, it is not an industry that is exempt when it comes to booby traps. One of the most common is the trap that Ken Jerald fell into.

Jerald was an experienced, enthusiastic senior vice president of marketing for a large, prestigious national real estate company. During his four years with the company, he had initiated numerous innovative sales plans, and was recognized in the industry as one of the bright, young up-and-coming executives.

In his position, Jerald made daily contact with vendors who sold everything from stationery to signage. He was in a powerful position, that also enabled him to give the final okay in the awarding of contracts worth hundreds of thousands of dollars.

Between his marketing position and the contracts he awarded, Jerald was the center of attention. Vendors and others in the industry, constantly sought his advice, and whenever they could—although it was not company policy—they tried to wine and dine him.

Jerald was at the top with one exception. He had fallen into disfavor with his boss, and the relationship between the two worsened every day. Jerald began to talk to vendors and others, always posing the same question—if he opened his own sales and marketing firm, would they be interested in utilizing him? He knew the industry, and those in it. He knew how to create and market winning products and services for the thousands of real estate sales associates—the prime customers of his company—who were in it.

The answer he received from everyone was "yes, of course, we would consider retaining you." Jerald began to calculate. He divided vendors and acquaintances into three categories that ranged from (1) those who would definitely give him business, (2) those who were not sure or were on the fence, and (3) those who would not.

After a month of figuring he made a decision. If only half of those he had in category 1 came through, his income would be doubled. The following week, he gave three weeks notice. The time would enable him to reapproach everyone in category 1 and get a firm commitment.

The next day, Jerald began to make the calls. The enthusiastic welcome he received confirmed his belief. He did notice one slight change. Whenever he told a prospect that he would be leaving his firm within a month, their voices changed. They became subdued. It was as if he had said he was being fired, instead of going into business for himself.

Nevertheless, Jerald continued his plan. At the end of his three weeks, he tacked on a week's vacation, which gave him time to recall the prospects, set up appointments, prepare proposals, and sign up business.

The three weeks passed, Jerald started his vacation, and judiciously started making calls the first morning of his last hiatus. Suddenly, he found that prospects were not as positive, when it came to sitting down and working out agreements. A number were willing to talk, but they never seemed to have time on their calendar.

Jerald kept making the calls. By the time his week's vacation was up, he had only managed to make two appointments. Everyone else was busy and asked him to call back in a week or two or the following month. Disappointed but undaunted, Jerald kept the appointments and found that the two firms did not have need for his services. The appointments were mostly out of courtesy.

Depressed, Jerald returned to his apartment and, once again, pulled out his plan. He began to scratch off names and revise his estimated income stream. The new figure was nowhere close to the old.

INITIAL CAPITAL

Dan Potter knows the feeling well and recognizes the mistake that Jerald made. "When you are employed and calling people it is one story. But when you leave your company and are out in the cold world with no company for leverage, it is another. Jerald should have planned for the reception he received. And, he should have put aside enough funds to last him six months to a year."

Jerald actually did. He had nearly a year's worth of capital put aside, and he almost needed every penny because it took him four months to generate his first client, and three more before he was in the black.

That was not the case with the consultants in this book, but as Potter cautions, "you never know about the reception you are going to receive. You may think you have a great idea, but don't be carried away by the reaction you get from people. Many prospective clients are prone to saying 'that's a great idea' until it comes time for them to put their money on the table or sign a contract. The same, incidentally, is true of relatives. They can be your biggest booster, but remember they usually are not retaining your services, either."

There is no better example of the importance of thorough research than an entrepreneur named Don Kracke. More than a decade ago, Kracke and his wife lived in San Francisco. One afternoon, they found themselves driving alongside a cablecar, and in back of a vintage Volkswagon "Bug." Pasted all over the "Bug" were paper flowers. Kracke and his wife laughed at the sight, but when they returned home they began to think about it. Flowers. Everyone in San Francisco loved them. Maybe the stickers were a good idea. Perhaps they had money-making potential.

The next day, Kracke and his wife spent the morning cutting out flowers from multi-colored paper. On the back, they put a glue-like substance, which would allow anyone to affix the flower to a wall, automobile, or whatever. Kracke and his wife made dozens of the stickers, and then went to the local department store. They traveled up and down the aisles, searching for a display. They were looking for any merchandising piece that could hold the stickers they were making. Finally, they found a rack that held paper cutouts, packaged in a plastic wrapper, and hung by a small hook onto the rack.

The Krackes returned home, took the colored flowers to a local plastics manufacturer, and asked if he could package them with an eye on the top of the plastic so it could be hung from a rack. The manufacturer supplied Kracke with a half-dozen of the packages, each filled with the colored flowers.

Next, Kracke and his wife started knocking on the doors of neighbors. They showed them the package, opened one, pulled out the flowered stickers, and asked if the neighbor would be willing to buy one and, if so, how much would they be willing to pay.

The "yes" answers coupled with a high dollar figure, were exactly what Kracke wanted to hear. The following morning he called and made an appointment to see the buyer at the local department store. Kracke came in the buyer's office with a half-dozen of the packages, opened one, pulled out one of the flowers, and explained how they were used. At first, the buyer laughed. But, Kracke continued. He told the buyer about his research, and the fact that more than 80 percent of the consumers in the area had indicated they would buy a package and pay $X.

The buyer was hesitant, but Kracke persisted. Finally, the buyer gave in to Kracke. He agreed to put two dozen of the packages in on consignment. They would hang on one of the racks near the front of the store. But, if they were not sold within 10 days, the items would be removed.

Kracke was ecstatic. And, for good reason. The packages sold out in 48 hours, and the buyer was frantically on the telephone asking for more. Thus, the famous "Ricky-Ticky-Stickys," the paste-on flowers that became a two-year fad throughout the country, were born. In just over two years, Kracke sold more than $3 million of flowers.

Today, when he looks back, he credits much of the success of the item to the research he and his wife did. They not only surveyed buyers, but they carefully scoured the department store to see what kind of merchandise racks were already in existence. Kracke knew it would be impossible to get any store to take on another display. But, he would have an excellent chance of placing the product if he could use a display that was already in-store.

"Ricky-Ticky-Stickys" are an excellent example of a product that was well-researched. Kracke did not let his enthusiasm for the product carry him away. He asked others pertinent questions, and test-marketed the product, too (at the department store). When everything worked, he rolled it out across the country.

HOW TO OPEN DOORS

Consultants face the same challenges. Before any prospective practitioner goes into business, he or she should test the waters. Survey potential clients, not just friends. Potter went through the market testing phase. "You no longer have a company name to open the door for you," he points out. "When you go into business, it is your name that has to open doors."

Potter remembers conversations he had with prospective clients, when he was evaluating the possibilities of opening a search firm. They were all positive; people were excited. "But I never knew for sure if I was going to get the business until I actually opened, made calls and appointments, and signed my first client. The same is true of any consulting field or, for that matter, any product or service.

"This is a great business, but prospects are not the same as clients. Prospects may say many nice things to you—however, the key is whether they will sign on the dotted line. Don't count on the income until you actually see it. Don't count on relationships you made at your company. Wait and see how many become clients before you start counting the income."

Potter tested. Kracke tested. Jerald did not. Every consultant should be doing adequate research before they open. There are numerous techniques that can be utilized to determine if there is a market for your services. First, look around. Study the companies in your area. Are they outsourcing? Check with the local chamber of commerce. They will be able to tell you if firms have been laying off workers, and contracting to outsiders.

Every company is involved in an industry. Automobiles are in the automotive industry; Hospitals in the health care field. Consultants are, too. For instance, Potter does executive search for the health care industry. There are publications within that industry that report on it. They are called trade papers. Call a trade and ask the editor(s) questions. Is the area growing, shrinking? Is there outsourcing going on? Do they have any forecast as to what will happen in the next few years? Is the industry growing? To find the names of trades, visit the local library and ask for a publication called Bacon's Publicity Checker. Bacon's carries the names and telephone numbers of virtually every trade paper in the country. Pick out two or three in your proposed industry, and call.

Call the local newspaper. Ask for the editor, and pose the same questions. Research is critical. It does not take a professional market researcher to dig up facts, and determine where an industry is going, and if it is promising for a consultant. Research is not going to guarantee whether your field will be lucrative or your business profitable, but it will give you insight into what's happening.

THE OVERSELLING HAZARD

Overselling/underselling impacts every industry, and there are few things that irritate a client more. The auto mechanic who promises your car will be back in four hours, and fails to deliver it for a day or longer; the printer who promises a job in two days, and does not finish for a week; the repairman who promises the computer is fixed, leaves the premises, and five minutes later the system goes down again. Every consumer has experienced one of these frustrating episodes, or something similar. You know the anger and feelings that develop, and the vow that you will never use that repairperson/printer/computer specialist again.

In the service business there are few things that can damage a business more than overpromising/underdelivering. However, for the consultant the temptation is always there. While competing for business, every consultant at one time or another, is tempted. It is a dangerous practice that can lead to a destroyed relationship and, worst of all, a client who will destroy your reputation.

BUILDING BUSINESS, NOT RELATIONSHIPS

Notre Dame football coach Lou Holtz tells the story of a clerk at a Hilton Hotel that Holtz ran into one evening. Holtz had traveled all day, and was due in Chicago for a speaking engagement the following morning. He arrived at the Hilton about 2 A.M., and thought he had a reservation when he asked the clerk for his room.

The clerk answered abruptly that Holtz did not have a reservation. Holtz argued, their voices got louder, and finally the football coach decided that in the best interests of all parties, he would leave. He did and found a hotel room elsewhere.

Holtz, however, never forgot the Hilton and the rude clerk, especially since the hotel's advertising had been balleyhooing the courtesy and great service at each of its hotels. Holtz addresses more than 50 large groups at conventions each year, and one of the things he discusses in great length is "treating others as you would like to be treated." And, at each of those gatherings, some holding upwards of 3,000 business travelers, he tells the story about the Hilton hotel and how he was treated—and names the hotel chain.

He shows businesspeople in the audience that when you treat someone badly clients may never forget it. They also make sure that everyone they come in contact with does not forget it, either.

Holtz grins when he relates the tale, and he closes it by relating a conversation he had with Mr. Hilton, the hotel chain's chief executive, who cringes each time he hears the story. The most damaging thing that can happen to a product and/or service is poor word-of-mouth by a customer.

FAILURE TO DELIVER

Not delivering cost the hotel chain one unhappy customer, and it damaged its reputation with tens of thousands of business travelers; travelers that Holtz reached each time he spoke. Rarely will one client reach tens of thousands of a consultant's prospects, but an unhappy customer will reach enough to impact a consultant and his company.

Overpromising and underdelivering definitely creates unhappy clients. Never overpromise, even in the heat of competition and trying to sign a prospect. If anything, the best tact is to underpromise and overdeliver. If it will take five days to do the research and put a proposal together, tell the client it will take six days. Give yourself an extra day. Then, if the proposal is delivered a day early, the prospective client will be pleased.

Delivering early, leaves a positive impression on the prospect. The consultant kept their word and delivered. That's a sign of reliability, a characteristic that clients require regardless of the service they are utilizing. If the consultant delivered the proposal early, perhaps he might do the same when he gets the job.

THE LISTENING FACTOR

Reliability is only one critical skill a consultant needs to be successful. If there were another near the top of the list, it would be the ability to listen. Jay Morgan knows why.

Morgan had a successful, independent advertising agency, and one of his largest clients was a theater chain. For several years, he had worked well with the marketing director of the chain, and the two saw things in a similar manner when creating campaigns.

Not everything lasts. One summer, the marketing director left the organization and went to another company. In his place, the chain hired a young, opinionated, aggressive executive. The advertising consultant met several times with the new marketing chief, and on each occasion the executive clearly spelled out what he wanted from the consultant's agency.

Following their meetings, the practitioner would return to his office, and work up another plan. Each time he returned, the marketing chief rejected them. Finally, after three months, the marketing director called the practitioner into his office, and severed the relationship.

It was not until months later—when a new advertising agency began airing a campaign for the chain—that the old agency president saw what was wrong. The new campaign was totally different from the one he had designed. But, it was quite familiar. The marketing director had outlined it every time the two met. Unfortunately, when the consultant returned to his office, he never remembered what the marketing director had asked. He was too focused on the campaigns he had run for the old director. He never listened to the new director.

Listening ranks as one of the most valuable skills a consultant can have. It can be a great plus or an enormous pitfall. More consultants lose business because they heard what the client said, but they did not listen.

A consultant can differ with a client, and offer other options as well as his opinion, but the cardinal sin is to blot out what the client is saying: To fail to listen.

Carol Beekman maintains one reason for the emergence of the female consultant is because of their ability to listen. That may or may not be true. Regardless of whether it is, the critical point to remember is that in order to be successful, a consultant has got to do more than hear the client—they have to listen.

Of all the consultants, Mike Green explains the next pitfall best. It is a simple one that every present and potential consultant knows well, and tries to avoid—failure to market your services.

LACK OF MARKETING

Every consultant knows the importance of marketing, but what frequently happens is a practitioner gets four or five clients, their time is taken up doing the work, and suddenly they are not marketing. "Most of us," says Green, "would rather consult than sell, so it does not take much for us to drop our marketing efforts when we are busy with clients. One day, however, you run out of projects, look up, and your client base has deteriorated. Before you get back on track it can take weeks. But, you still have to pay the bills."

Regardless of time pressures, marketing should be a priority. It might take the form of direct mail, telephone calls or letters. Some consultants set aside six or seven calls every day. They may be previous customers, or they could just be cold calling. Either way, they make the calls on a regular basis. Generating business is often as much a "law of averages" as anything else. The more you prospect, the greater the chance you have of opening a door. Whatever marketing process is put in place, it should be one that is done on a regular basis.

Potter says he has been fortunate. His practice has been filled with clients since he started, and he did little marketing aside from his initial campaign. Still, in the back of his mind he is worried. What if he runs out of his current projects? Where would he be?

Marketing to previous customers is frequently ignored. The consultant completes a project, and forgets about the customer. But, it is as important to drop a note or make a telephone call to a past client, as it is to a prospective customer.

Previous customers know the quality of work that your company can produce, and there are no better references. One technique is simply to call a previous client who was pleased with the project that was done, and simply ask them if they know of anyone else who might be in the market for a similar project. It is surprising how many names will pop up.

Past customers are extremely valuable. Mail order experts would say they are worth their weight in gold. Statistics show that if a client spent $10,000 with a consultant the first time, there is an excellent chance the client will spend an equivalent amount the next time around. Mail order mavens know the value of these satisfied customers. They are willing to break even on the first sale, just to get the prospect's name. That's why many firms market return address stickers and are even willing to sell them to consumers—through the mail—at a loss. They want the consumer's name. They know if the person bought once, there is a better than even chance they will buy again.

Keeping in touch on a regular basis, long after the project is completed, is one way of ensuring a second sale.

Regardless of marketing efforts, clients will never appear magically at the door, nor will referrals. Prospective clients (and others who can lead you to clients), have to be able to see you are a skilled, capable consultant before they will recommend you. They have to see and hear about your accomplishments. And, you have to ask them for those referrals.

Take a tip from the real estate industry. Every agent who ever goes through sales training learns one thing: Ask customers, neighbors, friends, relatives one question, "Do you know anyone who wants to buy or sell real estate?"

The recommendations and referrals will come when people feel confident about your abilities. That means clients, friends, or acquaintances have to know about your successes and accomplishments. The consultant has to keep them informed. It might be through reprints of positive newspaper articles, short notes ("thought you might be interested in the enclosed") that are affixed to articles that are of interest, and anything else the consultant finds in newspapers or magazines that is of value. The consultant has to keep the line open and build the relationship. Then the referrals will come.

THE BUSINESS SKILL FACTOR

Opening a practice is not just a matter of an individual hanging out a shingle, marketing services, writing proposals and collecting money. Consulting is a business, and it has to be run like one. Ask Chase Revel.

Revel is a name known to many in the entrepreneurial field. He started *Entrepreneur Magazine* with a $44 investment, and built it into a $15 million a year enterprise. At the height of its success, it was publicly held, and media throughout the country were clamouring to talk to the talented entrepreneur who had skillfully built the publishing empire.

Unfortunately, almost as fast as it was built, *Entrepreneur* came crashing down. It all started when Revel took off for a three-month vacation, and left several individuals in charge. When he came back, the magazine was in debt to the IRS, creditors, and consumers. In less than six months, a fabulous, enormously profitable enterprise had fallen.

What happened? Revel explains that *Entrepreneur* was a magazine, but more than that it was a business. Businesses have to be run in a business-like manner. Accounts have to be balanced, bills have to be paid, taxes reconciled, leases signed and negotiated, overhead monitored, and cash flow checked.

While Revel was out marketing, no one was taking care of business. The people he had left responsible for it failed to do the right things. All the sales in the world will not make a company, if it collapses at the business end.

Some have the wrong idea about what makes a business profitable. They look at sales, and when expenses rise, they presume the answer is in increased sales. That is not always the case. Recently, a national study was done of the real estate industry in an effort to determine what makes one realtor's practice profitable, and another—virtually in the same location with the same sales—marginal or unprofitable.

For years, the industry surmised that the difference in profits was due to some offices giving a higher percentage to agents (per sale) than others. In other words, one office might give an agent 60 percent of the commission, while another 90 percent. The prevailing wisdom forecast that the office that gave the highest percentage of commission was going to show the lowest profit—assuming sales of both offices were relatively equal.

When the study was finished, however, it turned out that commission split had nothing to do with profitability. What did was the business skills of the broker/manager who ran the office. How well they controlled expenditures was what determined the profitability of the company.

The same is true of consulting. Some practitioners sell one client after another, and wonder why they are not making more money. The reason: They are not running the enterprise like a business. They are not paying attention to the business end of the practice.

There are consultants who have trouble with business. But they have to realize it, and compensate for their weaknesses. Hire a professional accountant if there is problem with bookkeeping; a technology specialist if there is a problem with the computer; an advertising agency if there is difficult with ads that must be placed.

THE CAPITAL TRAP

Equally as disastrous as failure to pay attention to the business side of the practice is a lack of capital. Many consultants create unrealistic plans, and believe they will be able to register black ink within 60 to 90 days. Although this happens, and it did with each of the consultants in this book, it is not common.

Most of the time, entrepreneurs launching a business tend to underestimate the funds necessary to get and keep the enterprise going. Practitioners should have at least six months of capital set aside, and a year's supply is safer.

The consultants should look upon new ventures as enterprises that will not breakeven or generate enough clients for at least a year. If it happens sooner, fine.

For those who spread their capital too thin, new ventures can be disasters. Some of the best examples of what can happen when an enterprise is shy of capital are in the product field. But services run into the same difficulties. A few years ago, a fledgling record label was producing its first hit record. The record became a huge hit, and distributors and retailers throughout the country created an enormous demand.

The record label was undercapitalized, and the owner did not have enough money to press additional copies, but he convinced the manufacturing plant to advance him the funds. He would pay them back in 30 days. The label obtained additional credit from printers, shipping companies, and advertising agencies. They hired promotion people to get more airplay for the record, and the promotion people agreed to give him the 30 to 60 days he needed to pay bills.

Orders mounted, and shipments increased. From one million, orders came in for another 100,000, 200,000, and so on. During one 90-day period, the label shipped 2.5 million copies, and the record hit the top of the charts—number one.

Executives at the label should have been ecstatic, but instead their concern grew. Distributors who promised payment in 30 to 60 days were not sending any money. When the bookkeeper called, he was told large retailers had not paid their distribution bills, as yet. It would be another 30 days before they could get him any dollars.

The pressing facility began to call, asking for money. So did printers, promotion people, and every vendor to who the label had promised payment. The numbers of impatient people grew, but there was no money.

At the six-month mark, no money had been collected and in the end the vendors took the label president to court, forced him into bankruptcy, and the company was liquidated for a minimal amount of money. Eventually, the creditors collected 15 cents for each dollar owed. The label president, despite having one of the biggest hits of the year, walked away without a dime.

Months later, he looked back at the fiasco and wondered how it happened. How could he have lost when he had one of the biggest-selling records of the year? He failed to plan what would happen if he had a hit record. How much capital would he need?

In consulting, the same oversight is possible. A practitioner can open an office, and fail to set aside enough capital. Even if they generate several clients, the breakeven point may require one or two more. It takes time to build a business, and undercapitalization has ruined more than its share of promising enterprises.

IMPORTANCE OF SIGNED PROPOSALS

Another pitfall waiting to ensnare the consultant, is failure to submit a proposal that both parties agree to and sign. Proposals are not just selling tools. They are mini-contracts, and they protect the client as well as the consultant. If the client has a question as to what the project entailed, it is spelled out in the proposal. If the consultant gets half-way through the project, and the client asks about an element that was never discussed, the proposal is back up for the consultant.

Proposals improve communication between the client and consultant, and they help eliminate misunderstandings. Handshakes are fine, but they are forgotten when disagreements emerge over what the project actually entailed. The proposal keeps the assignment and relationship on track.

IMPORTANCE OF COMMUNICATION

Once the project is underway, one of the major causes of a problem with clients is too little or no communication. Some consultants fail to communicate frequently because they feel that what has happened is inconsequential. Nothing is too small to report. It is better to over-communicate. Nothing illustrates this better than the project a noted financial consultant had a few years ago. The financial consultant felt that small, seemingly insignificant things he found did not have to be relayed to the client. They could be summarized and reported at the end of the project, although some were impacting the company's profits.

The consultant was in the midst of an extensive audit for the client, a well-known jewelry store in Beverly Hills. Every day he seemed to discover another minor discrepancy in the financial procedures that had been established. However, he did not want to bother the owner with it.

Finally, after the consultant had been on the job for nearly three weeks, a frustrated owner walked into the office one evening after the store closed, and started going through the books and procedures himself. Within minutes, he found the first discrepancy that the consultant had noted. It was described and written in the margin of the financial procedures manual the company had put together.

The owner turned another page, and found another note, and so on. Before he was finished, he had found a half-dozen discrepancies that the financial consultant had uncovered.

The owner's anger was evident as he left the facility. The next morning, the first thing he did was call the consultant and fire him. The consultant never understood what had happened. He failed to understand that the owner had hired him not only to uncover problems, but communicate them as well.

Failure to provide the client with ongoing communication has cost many practitioners a project. Clients want to hear from the consultant on a regular basis. They want to know how the project is going, and what the status is of it. Communication can take the form of a simple note sent on a weekly basis, a telephone call made each Friday to bring the client up-to-date, or a written addendum to a weekly bill.

The more often you communicate, the smoother the project will go. If something is not working correctly, let the client know. Do not leave surprises for the end of the project.

Branberg often sends a bill on a weekly basis, and each invoice contains a summary of what has happened, and what is planned. He may also telephone the client, and provide them with the same information, or if they are on-site, he will visit the CEO (Chief Executive Officer) or whomever is responsible for bringing him in to handle the project. Branberg never misses an opportunity to bring the client up-to-date. There is no such thing as too much information.

HOW TO BILL

Related to communication is billing. There should never be any surprises. Each expense, for instance, should be explained and backed up with receipts. Regardless of the trust the client has, it should be established policy to have every expenditure detailed with the proper verification.

Hours—if that is the way the client is billed—on the job should be detailed, too, and time frames (why, what was done, who did it) for each phase of the project should be spelled out.

SUMMARY

Pitfalls are present in every business and each consulting practice. But, if the practitioner is conscious of them, a consulting practice will not only be one of the most profitable businesses imaginable, but the smoothest running as well.

CHAPTER 7

SAMPLE PROPOSALS, DIRECT MAIL, AND OTHER KEY WRITTEN INGREDIENTS

There are dozens of reasons why a client decides to hire one particular consultant over another, and although relationships and reputation play an enormous role, the written materials—from proposals to pitch letters—play a critical part in that ultimate decision.

One of the most important written documents is the proposal. It can contain everything from the consultant's background to a step-by-step analysis of the problem and the implementation of the solution. They are carefully worded, easy-to-read, and can make the difference in whether the consultant gets the business.

Figure 7.1 (on pp. 156–167) is a proposal provided by a consultant to help clarify the role of the practitioner and what he will be doing. The names were changed for reasons of confidentiality, however, it gives you a good idea of how a detailed, bullet-point proposal should look; the areas it should stress; and the details it contains.

This proposal was put together following several meetings between the consultant, the client, and other members of the prospect's company. Notice, there is only a minimal amount of information on the consultant's firm (p. 164), primarily because the prospect has already met the practitioner, gone through several meetings with the consulting firm, and has already been given background information.

The contents make it easy for the client to flip to any section, and the bullet points make it equally as simple to find subjects. The Introduction is an "executive summary," in that it summarizes the problem as the consultant sees it following her interviews with the client. If there is any misunderstanding about what the prospect expects, it will surface in this area of the proposal.

Notice one other thing—the clarity and ease with which a client can read the proposal. There is no fluff or attempt to dazzle the prospect with verbiage. The proposal gets to the problem, offers the solution and the cost. And, it is all in easy-to-understand English.

The cost and price analysis—that is, the bottom line—is at the end. By the time the client gets to the cost/price, the consultant assumes that the pages preceding it have enough meat/content to not only confirm that the consultant is going in the right direction, but the ideas the prospect have read are creative enough to warrant the fees.

The second proposal (Figure 7.2 on pp. 168–171) is closer to a "draft" proposal, which a number of consultants utilize. (It, too, has had the names changed for confidentiality.) This proposal was written following two (each lasting about two hours) meetings with the client. From those meetings, the consultant developed an understanding of what she thought the problem was and what the client needed. This draft is submitted to see if the consultant is on-track. It is given to the prospect before anything like the proposal in Figure 7.1 is written.

FREE EXPOSURE LEADS TO CLIENTS

Consultants will unanimously tell you that there is no one form of advertising that brings in clients. However, writing and placing news releases has opened doors and prompted inquiries from prospective clients. Public relations (PR), or publicity, carries credibility with it in the form of an independent endorsement from a third party (media). If the media thinks enough of this consultant to write about them, maybe we (the prospective clients) should be talking to his company.

Four standard PR releases that were put together by consultants are shown in Figures 7.3 to 7.6. The names have been left blank, however, any consultant could use the same format, insert their information, and have a news release.

Figure 7.3 (on p. 172) is about a free seminar. The release was sent to local newspapers, as well as to trade papers in the hospitality industry, that is, publications that are usually read by those in the hotel business.

The sales training consultant who wrote this release is targeting his audience. Anyone in the hotel industry who reads it in a hotel trade journal or on the business page of the local newspaper could be a candidate for attending the seminar. The "free" aspect of the seminar is designed to bring in as many potential clients as possible. In 90 minutes, the consultant can give attendees a great deal of valuable information and, at the same time, not go into detail. The goal: Spark enough interest from seminar attendees to open some doors and develop prospective clients.

The news release in Figure 7.4 (on p. 173) is similar to the previous release. It is an hour-long session designed to spark interest and open the doors of prospective clients. It, too, is free.

Notice, this release has a slight twist. It is sponsored by the local chamber of commerce. Chambers always put on business seminars or co-sponsor them. It is one of their responsibilities as an organization created to support the business community.

Sponsorship by the chamber gives the speaker credibility. It also sets them us as an authority. And, most of the time, a news release that is submitted by the chamber, has an excellent chance of being published.

The chamber release is followed by one that was written by the Sterns, and sent to the trades (human resource journals). It is not a release that would be sent to all media, since the "SourceFinder" only relates to those people in the human resource field. Additionally, the Sterns also sent it to the local chamber publication. In the trade area, Bacon's Publicity Checker (Magazine Directory) carries a complete list of trades that are targeted to human resource professionals. Some are national, others local (see Figure 7.5 on pp. 174–175).

Figure 7.6 (on p. 176) is standard in most industries. It is an announcement (of a company's opening) release and is sent to both local media as well as trade press. For instance, the opening of this executive search firm, could be sent to local newspapers (where the consultant has his offices), the local chamber for publication in its newsletter, and to trade papers that reach the consultant's potential market. If, for instance, this release were sent by Dan Potter, the executive search consultant who deals in the health care field, releases would also be sent to all trade publications that covered the health care field. These journals are, of course, read by Potter's potential audience.

THE POWER OF THE LETTER

Some years ago, a well-known humorist wrote a book that garnered rave reviews by critics throughout the country. It was not his first book, but it was one that attracted a great deal of attention.

A few weeks after it was published, he received the following, good-natured, amusing note from a friend:

> Dear _____,
>
> By some miracle you have published a book which is not second rate. Please send me twelve copies at once.
>
> Sincerely,

Without hesitation, the author fired back a note to his friend:

> Dear _____,
>
> By some miracle, you can find those twelve copies at Brentano's.
>
> Yours very truly,

Letter writing need not be long and drawn out in order to make a point. Consultants do not have to write two- and three-page letters in order to communicate with clients or prospects. Most people have little time for reading, thus the shorter the letter, the more effective it is going to be. The following four notes are brief communiques that were sent from consultants to prospects or clients. Each has its own point.

> Dear (name of prospect):
>
> Just a short note to let you know I am taking the plunge . . . I have just opened a management consulting office in (name of area, city, community, etc.).
> If I can ever be of service, please let me know.
> In the meantime, hope all's well and business is booming.
>
> Sincerely,

Carol Beekman composed a similar announcement when she opened her communications/PR practice, and enclosed a business card with each. The response she got from that one mailing (she covered people in her rolodex, plus anyone else she knew), generated enough business to keep her busy for a year.

Beekman and other consultants point out that "we think everyone knows we have gone into business, but that is not necessarily true. It is up to us to let them know." This short note, and Beekman's announcement are two ways of doing it.

> Dear _____,
>
> Thought you might be interested in the enclosed. In ran in last (day) (name of newspaper, magazine or publication).
>
> Sincerely,

This letter to a prospect from a consultant usually includes some item that the practitioner spotted and thought would be of interest to one of his prospects or clients.

It also keeps the doors open and the relationship building. And it could arrive at exactly the same time the prospect/client is thinking about a consulting project that they need to get done. It keeps the consultant's name in front of the prospect, and shows the businessperson that the consultant has been thinking about the client's company.

Dear _____ ,

Congratulations! Just heard about the promotion. Well deserved.

Sincerely,

A simple note with a powerful impact. Everyone has an ego, and recognizing someone for something they have done is impactful. Even if the promotion is commonly known, it never hurts to send a congratulatory note, one of the most powerful notes anyone can write.

Dear (name of prospect):

Thought you might be interested in the enclosed, which ran in the business section last week.
. . . Well deserved.

Sincerely,

This is an example of a consultant reading about someone's promotion (award, etc.), cutting out the article, and sending it to the prospect.

Every successful consultant does periodic, scheduled mailings. They may be monthly or quarterly, but they are scheduled. The mailings may be in the form or articles the consultant has found and deemed worthwhile, or just a note saying congratulations on your company's fifth (or whatever) anniversary.

Mike Green believes there is nothing more powerful than regular mailings. None of his mailings are designed to close a sale, but they are structured to open the door in the event the prospect is thinking of hiring a consultant. Green, and others, keep their name in front of the client.

Letters are not difficult to write. Good ones have the same, simple structure, regardless of length. It is called "AIDA"—Attention, Interest, Desire, Action. Or, they have a structured beginning, middle, and end. AIDA means to open with something that will get the reader's attention. It could be as simple as "Congratulations" or "Remember our meeting the other day." The best attention getting openings involve the reader. "How would you like to double your company's profits?"

Lines such as that are guaranteed to get a reader's interest. Interest is the second part of a letter. It is generated by the opening. For instance, if a sales trainer wrote "How would you like to increase the productivity of your sales force by 50 percent without spending any additional funds?" That would intrigue most sales managers.

Attention and interest are followed by desire (on the part of the reader to find out more) and finally—in some letters—a call to action; to do something. AIDA is the format for most sales letters, and every piece of correspondence from a consultant to a prospect is a sales letter, whether it is selling a particular service or not.

The ideal structure—open with an interesting line; follow the attention-getter with something of interest (to the client), build desire and, finally, the desire to act.

Not every letter seeks action. Some are just short congratulatory notes, and require nothing more than the recipient remembering the sender and appreciating the note.

The format for correspondence of this type:

- Beginning
- Body
- Conclusion (end)

Simple. Your letter should read like a story. It should have an interesting beginning, the purpose or message should be in the body, and the conclusion (which can be as simple as "Sincerely" ends the note). For instance, the four different notes to prospects (above) are examples of simple beginning, body and conclusion notes. They are short, easy-to-read notes, but each has the same format.

DUAL MESSAGES IN LETTERS

Every letter carries two messages—the literal one, and the one that the form, structure and language of the note relays. For example, a letter sending a reprint of an interesting (from the client's perspective) article to a prospect, may be straightforward and the article is appreciated. But, if the consultant has two or three misspelled words in the note, that sends another message to the prospect—this person is not too careful, not thorough, and they may treat my project the same way. Thus, letters are not only a powerful marketing tool, but they can impact the reader in more ways than just one.

NEWS TWIST TO BROCHURES

During a good portion of the 1980s, every consultant's brochure looked like it was competing for an award. There were four-, five-, and six-color productions; brochures with tri-folds and tick folds; pockets in the back, or pockets in the middle; clever artwork, and expensive photography. It was all done to relay an image to the buyer (prospect), and although some consultants still using glossy, high design brochures, they are fading quickly. In fact, only a few of the top 10 consultants utilize a brochure.

Dan Potter has a simple tri-fold he put together to hand out at trade shows; Rudy Dew has an inexpensive, 8½ × 11 inch, full-size, one-color, four-page brochure that would not win any art awards, but it does contain pertinent facts about outplacement and Dew's services (see Figure 7.7 on pp. 177–180).

The typical brochure contains several key elements:

1. Something about your company; your background.
2. The services it offers and why those services are different (and better) than anyone else.
3. Any specialties you might offer.

If a consultant is going to put a brochure together, one thing should be remembered—aside from the copy that is inside, anything you send will connote a definite image of your company. If the brochure is slipshod, printed on cheap stock, and appears as if it were designed by a grammar school student, that can impact your business.

We are all impressionable, and if the brochure is the first contact a prospect has with your company, the way it looks is going to be the image the prospect has in their mind of your company. A good-looking, neat brochure says this consultant is the same way; a brochure that does not offer that image, can detract.

Other rules for brochures include:

1. If you use photographs, get a professional photographer.
2. Make sure the copy is written and edited with the client in mind. Tell what you can do for them. Talk about solving needs.
3. Use a professional designer. Even if the brochure is inexpensive, a professional can add a touch with shades, screens and duotone that will keep the brochure inexpensive but effective, too.
4. Keep the copy short, bulleted if possible. No one has time to read.
5. Make the type style something that is easy to read, too. The designer can help in this area.
6. If possible, develop a logo and use it on the brochure, as well as your stationery.

Remember, brochures, letterhead and anything that goes out of your office to clients reflects back on your company. You may be the best consultant in your field, but if the printed materials do not give that impression, they can hinder more than help your marketing efforts.

THE ALTERNATIVE TO THE BROCHURE

The trend to simpler, less expensive brochures is well-established, but in some cases consultants are even abandoning the inexpensive productions in favor of straight-forward, "resume"-type letters.

For instance, Stern has put together several different fact sheets. The first (Figure 7.8 on p. 181) tells "About Stern & Associates." It has bold-faced points, and makes it easy for the client to follow.

Stern has another document, a narrative (see Figure 7.9 on pp. 182–183) that is followed by an impressive list of clients (Figure 7.10 on p. 184). He can send one (or all) to a client, depending upon the interest level.

Rudy Dew has done something similar (Figure 7.11 on p. 185). It is a narrative about his experience, and mentions a number of clients. When a consultant has prestigious clients, they can help sell others.

Figure 7.12 (on pp. 186–187) is a resume of the consultants that Dew has working with him, and their background and capabilities are impressive. This usually accompanies a letter to a prospect.

Mike Green has been extremely successful with the "qualifications" letter he sends (see Figure 7.13 on pp. 188–189). Green uses this in direct mail, and sends it to CEOs and other decision makers. He will send out 400 to 500 at a time, but will target the list. For example, he makes sure the CEOs are heading organizations with minimum sales of about $5 million.

In the 1980s, this approach would have been tough to utilize as a marketing tool, but today CEOs and other prospects, are not interested in expensive brochures as much as they are in qualifications. Green's hope is that the qualifications piece hits a CEO's desk at exactly the moment he has a consulting problem, and is thinking of hiring one.

Dew has created several other pieces that explain his business, what he does, and what he has to offer. They solve the problem that many prospects have of not quite understanding what a consultant does. For instance, if you mention the word "outplacement," decision makers would be familiar with it, however, most would not be able to tell you what the outplacement process consists of. The same is true of other consulting professions. Prospects are familiar with the name, but not the process.

Dew has a "Time Limited Program" (see Figure 7.14 on pp. 190–192) which may mean nothing to most clients, but thanks to a neat, bulleted handout, and another sheet that breaks down the two days, and a third that goes into greater depth in explaining what happens when, Dew's "Time Limited Program" has become something that clients can easily understand, and ask intelligent questions about.

Dew has an individual executive program (see Figure 7.15 on pp. 193–194) which he has broken down in a similar manner.

APPROACHING CLIENTS

At times, consultants get a telephone call from a prospective client who simply wants "more details." The consultant visits, gets some sketchy details and then puts together a follow-up letter (Figure 7.16 on pp. 195–200).

A variation of this letter—that is, one with less details—could be used by a consultant who wants to send something in advance of the first meeting with a client. In that case, the letter would include background and successful projects. It is not wise to quote fees (in writing) unless it happens to be part of the proposal, or the client requests it after the initial meeting. In an introductory letter, a consultant would not outline their methods in detail, either. Methods are something the client has to be sold on—and clients are not sold on a method until they "buy" the consultant, and that does not happen before the consultant/client have at least one or two meetings.

HOW TO SET YOURSELF APART

By authoring the "Stern's SourceFinder,"® the couple have developed a unique approach which sets them apart from all other consultants in their field. They are not only published authors, but anyone who buys the book is a potential lead—and client.

The "SourceFinder" (see Figure 7.17 on p. 201), has generated the pair numerous leads, and a reputation in the human resource community. Notice the benefits (see Figure 7.18 on p. 202) someone gets when the buy the "SourceFinder." One is a "free newsletter," which enables the Sterns to keep in touch with prospects.

Another intriguing technique he uses is the "Beyond the Source-Finder," a telephone consulting technique, which enables prospects to contact them without making a major commitment to consulting services. Once someone has made the telephone call, they are a prime prospect.

Figure 7.19 (on pp. 203–205) gives you an idea of why the "Source-Finder" has been a hit. Examine the detail of the entries and the benefits to those in the human resource field.

Aside from the "SourceFinder" being a valuable resource for those in HR, it is also an idea source for other consultants. Publishing a resource book or newsletter for a particular industry, can be a potent marketing tool.

And, it is exactly that for the Stern's.

HUGE COMPANY, INC.

PROPOSAL ADDRESSING:
THE DEVELOPMENT OF A JOB/SKILL
VALUE PROGRAM THAT COMPLEMENTS
A MARKET PRICING APPROACH
TO CASH COMPENSATION PLANNING
AND ADMINISTRATION

July 23, 199X

FIGURE 7.1.   Sample proposal.

TABLE OF CONTENTS

FIGURE 7.1.   (Continued.)

I

INTRODUCTION

HUGE COMPANY, INC. (HC) requested a proposal addressing the development and implementation of a job/skill value program that:

- supports *Performance Management*, and

- complements the market pricing focus adopted by the corporate Compensation Department.

Performance Management is a total cash compensation program that includes three components: an individual incentive, a team incentive, and base pay.

- The **two incentive compensation** components are highly dependent upon a thoughtful and sound business planning process.

- The **base pay** component is highly dependent upon:

  * the precise and accurate descriptions of skills, knowledge, and abilities related to jobs, and
  * the valid and reliable internal valuing and external pricing of skills and jobs.

This proposal addresses the provision of professional management consulting assistance to the Employee Development Division (ED) of the Main Divison (MD) and the Corporate Compensation Department. The consulting services include the identification and implementation of a methodology which permits internal and external values to be placed on jobs and/or skills, and therefore, a provide valid and reliable basis for base pay planning and administration.

ABC Consulting, Inc., (ABC) has chosen to use the term *job/skill value* as opposed to the traditional term "job evaluation". It is our understanding at this time, that HC has not decided whether to move towards a skill-based pay program or remain with a compensation program that uses job evaluation to place internal values on jobs and to compare them with the external marketplace.

Our term, *job/skill value*, focuses on line-of-sight value contributions to the overall business goals and is intended to allow HC the option to select a program that focuses on skill employment rather than on traditional job evaluation criteria. It is our understanding that HC is not necessarily wedded to any one methodology and is, therefore, open to identifying and selecting the methodology that best meets the base pay needs of *Performance Management* and the immediate and longer term human resources goals for fair and equitable cash compensation.

FIGURE 7.1.   (Continued.)

At this point, it is understood that *Performance Management* is being implemented as a pilot program within the Fast Line Department (Fast). Assuming that *Performance Managemnt* is successful it is intended that it be used as the cash compensation program for all personnel within MD. The methodology selected must be flexible and potentially be able to encompass a wide range of jobs and skills throughout MD and, possibly, all of HC.

The remainder of this proposal follows the outline requested in the Request for Proposal. Section II of this proposal document outlines our recommended Project Approach and Work Plan. Section III provides details of Project Staffing and a summary of our Consulting Firm's Experience. Section IV includes the Statement of Potential Conflict of Interest. Section V provides the Cost and Price Analysis requested.

If additional information is required, we would be happy to provide it.

ABC CONSULTING, INC.
PAGE 2

FIGURE 7.1.   (Continued.)

II

RECOMMENDED PROJECT APPROACH AND WORK PLAN

OBJECTIVE OF THE PROJECT

- To ensure that the base pay component of *Performance Management* is appropriately supported through the use of a job/skill value program that accurately, precisely, and properly assesses the internal and external value of jobs and/or skills as they contribute to the business success of HC.

The specific Project Objectives might be as follows:

- To identify the appropriate job/skill value methodology for HC to use as an integral part of its cash compensation planning and administration.

- To recommend an approach to implementing the selected job/skill value methodology to ensure cost-effective cash compensation planning and administration.

- To provide assistance in implementation of the selected job/skill value methodology.

SCOPE OF THE PROJECT

As indicated by the Objectives, the project has two major components: the selection of the methodology, and the implementation of the chosen methodology.

It is the belief of ABC that input and participation from the population most affected by a proposed human resources program should be included in the design and/or selection of most programs. This approach serves two purposes:

- (i)   the personnel involved can become ED's and corporate Compensation Department's "salesforce" for the program, and

- (ii)   issues that may be overlooked by staff and senior management are brought to the forefront and receive the necessary attention.

We are, therefore, recommending that HC select a *Value Team* to work with the consultants on this project.

The three phases outlined below provide an overview of our approach.

PHASE I: PLANNING AND DATA COLLECTION

It is assumed that the HC Project Team will consist of Ms. Gemima Everett, Ms. Dana Sepitt, Mr. Daniel Avon, an ED Analyst, Ms. Amy Consultant -- the Client Manager for ABC, and a representative from Major & Associates who currently coordinate the overall efforts of compensation planning for HC.

FIGURE 7.1.   (Continued.)

- The HC Project Team will agree upon the final details, deliverables, and deadlines for the project.

- The Project Team will select a *Value Team* to act as the advisors to the Project Team. The Value Team might consist of three managers -- one each from Rossmoor, San Juan and the field, and four supervisors and non-managers -- again one each from Rossmoor and San Juan, and two from the field. It would also be preferable to have two representatives from the compensation group of the Innovators who designed *Performance Management*.

The role of this Team would be threefold:

(i)   to provide input on the nature and type of information necessary to understand jobs and the skills needed to contribute to organizational success,

(ii)   to evaluate the recommendations of the consultants and provide input to ED and Corporate Compensation in order to aid in the selection of the Job/Skill Value methodology, and

(iii) to assist ED, Corporate Compensation and the consultants in developing and executing an implementation plan for the selected program.

The Consultants will meet with Mr. Daniel Avon and Ms. Dana Sepitt and representatives of ED to gain their individual understandings of job and skill value contributions to the success of HC and, specifically, MD.

- The Consultants will meet with the Value Team to develop an understanding of their collective and individual perspectives on job and skill value contributions to the success of MD and to *Performance Management*.

- The Consultants will meet with some or all of the members of the compensation group of the *Performance Management* Innovators. This meeting is to ensure that the compensation philosophy and base pay nuances of *Performance Management* are fully understood.

- The consultants will review, with Corporate Compensation, the current and proposed job and skill description formats to determine the type and nature of the information collected and documented to date.

- The consultants will summarize the Findings and Observations in a Preliminary Report to share with the Project Team and the Value Team.

PHASE II: SELECTION OF A JOB/SKILL VALUE PROGRAM

- The consultants will prepare a summary of the methodologies which would be readily available to HC. The summary will divide the options into broad categories and include an assessment of the strengths and weaknesses of each methodology. The benefits and cost-effectiveness to HC will be analyzed and presented as part of this summary.

FIGURE 7.1.   (Continued.)

At this stage, it is thought that there might be four options available to HC. These include:

(i) Develop a skill-based job value system that recognizes the internal and external value of skills employed to perform jobs satisfactorily. This approach may utilize a job family approach or it may identify the knowledge, skills, and abilities necessary to successfully accomplish various work processes. This could require that HC develops job/skill ladders that focus specifically on meeting customer service and business needs.

(ii) Develop a paired comparisons methodology that meets HC needs. This may use a job family or independent job approach.

(iii) Use **PRODUCT #1**, a proprietary automated job evaluation system developed originally for service industries. **PRODUCT #1** has six recommended compensable factors, however, the user company has the option to develop its own factors or to amend the existing factors as they relate to business plan success and the value system of the user company. The factors describe the internal relative value of jobs but are priced using market data.

(iv) Continue to use the current job evaluation program but amend its use to include market pricing criteria in defining and selecting benchmark jobs.

• The summary will first be presented to the Value Team and, subsequently, to the Project Team. The Value Team will be asked to provide feedback to the Project Team and, if appropriate, be asked to make a recommendation on the most appropriate methodology for determining job/skill value within the ***Performance Managemnt*** pilot group and, prospectively, to all MD jobs.

The Value Team will use previously established and agreed upon criteria to judge the methodologies. These criteria may include but not be limited to the following questions:

• is the system fair and defensible?

• does it support the aims and objectives of ***Performance Mangement***?

• does it allow market pricing to become a significant portion of the final judgement on job/skill price?

• is it possible to value most, if not all, HC jobs and skills?

• can the job/skill value criteria be communicated effectively?

• is it simple and uncomplicated to use and maintain?

• The final recommendations will be summarized in a report for the Project Team. The report will be formally presented by the Consultants along with estimated costs of implementation and maintenance.

FIGURE 7.1. (Continued.)

PHASE III: IMPLEMENTATION OF THE SELECTED JOB/SKILL VALUE METHODOLOGY

- Implementation will depend upon the methodology selected in Phase II.

  From an expense perspective, implementation may be as simple and inexpensive as choosing to continue with the current job evaluation methodology, but refining the definition and use of benchmarks as they relate to the use of external market data. Or, implementation may require the major time and expense of developing HC's own skills-based value plan.

  From a complexity perspective, continuing the current job evaluation program or the selection of **PRODUCT #1** are the least complex to implement. The development of a paired comparison or skill-based methodology may be kept relatively simple or may become as complex as HC wishes it be.

- The consultants role in implementation could range from one of consultative guidance for key planning and execution milestones to one of leading a development team. Again, we would see this as part of the decision-making process in Phase II.

- The consultants will certainly be involved in the review of the selected factors to ensure their reliability and validity.

- A key role of the consultants will be to ensure that the implementation process includes training to ensure non-discriminatory application of job/skill factors.

- The consultants will work with ED and Corporate Compensation to develop and execute a full and complete marketing and communication program.

DELIVERABLES

- A Methodology that recognizes internal value for jobs and/or skills employed.

- A Methodology that blends easily and effectively with market data analyses.

- Assistance on initial implementation, the nature of which will be dependent of the methodology .

- If selected, an automated program for continuous evaluation and system improvement.

TIME SCHEDULES

- ABC will begin work within two weeks of notification of acceptance of this or an amended proposal. Phases I and II will be completed by October 31, 1993 assuming that the necessary HC resources are readily available. The completion of Phase III which includes implementation of the selected program will depend upon the approach chosen.

FIGURE 7.1. (Continued.)

III

PROJECT STAFFING AND CONSULTING FIRM'S EXPERIENCE

- ABC is a 100% female owned California Corporation with a sound reputation for developing innovative human resources programs.

- The two principals each have twenty years of experience, primarily in management consulting with a human resources emphasis within a variety of industries both in the United States and in Europe. Ms. Consultant and Dr. Psychologist have each been with major national consulting firms and also built successful consulting practices. They have each delivered custom tailored programs for a wide variety of clients in a broad range of industries.

- The consultants bring fluency in organization design, job evaluation, cash compensation, and performance management to HC.

- A brief resume on each individual and buisness references are provided on the following pages.

ABC CONSULTING, INC.
PAGE 7

FIGURE 7.1.   (Continued.)

V

COST AND PRICE ANALYSIS

- Our estimate of professional fees to complete Phases I and II this project as described in Section II will range from $64,000 (sixty-four thousand dollars) to $70,000 (seventy thousand dollars). If there is any change to the approach we have outlined in Section II the estimated fees will be reviewed and a revised estimate provided.

   The total fee estimate provided in this proposal for this project as described in Section II will remain valid for a period of up to six months from the date of this proposal document.

- Expenses for travel, extraordinary report and graphics production, special mail and messenger and so forth, which are billed in addition, are estimated to be no more than 10% - 15% of professional fees.

- Invoices detailing consulting time and project-related expenses incurred the previous month are sent monthly and are payable upon receipt.

- If HC finds it necessary or desirable to terminate the services of ABC, it is free to do so and is only obligated to pay fees and expenses incurred up to that point.

CONSULTANT HOURLY BILLING RATES

The following listing contains the hourly billing rates for each member of the proposed consulting team. Consistent with HC terms and conditions, these rates include overhead and administrative costs.

Any Consultant	Client Manager	$250
Celect Genius	Senior Consultant	$200
Jolly Finance	Senior Consultant	$200
Keep Focused	Consultant	$125

FIGURE 7.1. (Continued.)

ESTIMATED* FEE ALLOCATION BY PHASE

	PHASE I Hours Fees		PHASE II Hours Fees		PHASE III Hours Fees
PRINCIPAL	36	$ 9,000	48	$12,000	To Be Determined
SENIOR CONSULTANT	44	$ 8,800	88	$17,600	To Be Determined
CONSULTANT	40	$ 5,000	96	$12,000	To Be Determined
TOTAL:	120	**$22,000**	216	**$36,400**	**To Be Determined**

NOTE: The fee allocation provided by Consultant, by phase is only an estimate at this time. It is our policy to remain flexible to client needs at all stages of a project. If this allocation by phase and/or by Consultant is found to be inappropriate once we have started the project, we reserve the right to reorganize our resources within the total fee quotation provided.

ESTIMATED EXPENSE ALLOCATION

AIRFARE	AUTO	HOTEL	FOOD	MILEAGE	OTHER
$ 2,000	$ 750	$ 2,500	$ 500	$ 1,000	<$3,000*

NOTE: The "other" expense estimate may include extraordinary report and/or graphics production or related project items. HC will be informed before there is any significant expenditure on items falling under "Other".

COST CONTROL MEASURES

- Our internal project control systems track all consultant and support staff time and direct expenses.

- Consistent with HC'S general terms and conditions, all overhead and administrative costs have been included in the professional fees.

- Our system enables us to generate invoices and provide documentation for all expenses consistent with HC requirements as presented in the project RFP.

- The Client Project Manager for ABC is responsible for ensuring the timely, cost-effective completion of all work tasks.

- HC will be responsible for ensuring that HC project team member time commitments are fulfilled.

FIGURE 7.1.   (Continued.)

INVOICE

Accounts Payable
HUGE COMPANY, INC.XXXX Waytogo Avenue
Rossmoor, CA XXXXX

Invoice Date	August 1, 199X	**Invoice Number**	0000
Purchase Order	N 0000000	**Project Number**	12-501-08
Page Number	1 of 1		

Consulting fees for Any Consultant ($250 per hour):
April 2 (8 hrs / Mtg-ED Mgrs/ Brunner Park) $ 2,000.00
April 27 (4 hrs / Mtg-ED, Project Admin / Whiteout City) 1,000.00

Consulting fees for Celect Genius ($200 per hour) :
May 14(8 hrs /100 Follow-up: Sams & Carter/Langhold Beach & Rosmoor) 1,600.00
June 15(6 hrs /100 Follow-up: Fish/Rossmoor) 1,200.00

Sub Total of Consulting Fees **5,800.00**

	AIRFARE	AUTO	HOTEL	FOOD	MILEAGE	OTHER	TOTAL
A. Consultant				189.39	456.40	30.80	676.59
C. Genius					21.84		21.84

Sub Total of Expenses: **$ 698.43**

Grand Total Fees and Expenses **$ 6,498.43**

TERMS: PAYABLE UPON RECEIPT

FIGURE 7.1. (Continued.)

July 14, 199X

Mr. Mark Image
Vice President
SORE BACKS Medical Center
XXXX Medical Street
London Heights, CA XXXXX

Dear Mark:

As requested, I have outlined an approach and an estimated fee cost to assist you and/or Stacy Green develop and implement a self-directed team process and a team compensation program for the OSM group of businesses.

As I see it at this point in time, there are three major pieces that need to be accomplished for the OSM to adopt new, productive processes and systems.
♦   Development of the cash compensation program.
♦   Development of the team process.
♦   Ongoing refinement and review of the team process and cash compensation program.

As you are aware, I favor an approach that includes asking a group of "users" to help design the programs. This group also becomes the principle "sales" force for implementation of the final product. While this approach is not the only one available, my experience has indicated that the final product (whatever it might be) is usually better received and more thoroughly developed.

I have described the recommended approach to be taken if we use a development group. If you wish to use another approach please do not hesitate to let me know and I can develop another proposal for you.

STEP 1:   DEVELOPMENT

This would entail selecting a small group of "users", typically called a Design Team, who are representative of levels and jobs that currently exist within the OSM. The initial task of the group would be to refine and ready for implementation, a compensation program that would include a number of cash components including base or core pay and individual and team variable pay.

FIGURE 7.2.   Letter proposal.

Mr. Mark Image
SORE BACKS Medical Center
July 14, 199X

Page 2

The second task would be to develop a team process for the "management" processes needed for a successful business. I have a number of examples that they can use and refine for specific use in the OSM.

STEP 2:   COMMUNICATION AND IMPLEMENTATION

The Design Team would be accountable for developing the communication process and for overseeing implementation. The development of compensation guidelines would be carried out by the Design Team with the assistance and support of Human Resources and the consultants.

STEP 3:   REFINING THE TEAM PROCESS

This step would include the facilitation needed for the work groups to learn and adopt team behaviors. Typically, this would be more intensive at first and taper off over time as teams become self-sufficient.

Each group would need separate facilitation and it would be my intention to train several SMMC people as facilitators. Facilitation skills are needed in-house if self-directed teams become the primary approach to business.

I think that monthly meetings with each team may be necessary for the first three months and then quarterly meetings for the remainder of the year. At the end of one year, the teams should be ready to continue without a facilitator. However, it is wise to have facilitators available to help teams through particularly difficult or political issues.

PROFESSIONAL FEES AND EXPENSES

Our professional fee structure consists of a usual charge for professional services of between $90.00 and $250.00 per hour depending upon the level and type of consultant used. This fee is charged only for the time we spend on a project and includes general administrative expenses, e.g. regular typing, regular mail and telephone calls.

FIGURE 7.2.   (Continued.)

Mr. Mark Image
SORE BACKS Medical Center
July 14, 199X

Page 3

Mark, the usual rate for your organization is $200 per hour with a maximum charge of eight hours for a day. If you decide to go ahead with this project, I am willing to lower my hourly rate to $150 per hour for this project only. The project tends to be highly labor intensive and I interested in helping you make the process work.

Given this, the estimate of fees is as follows:

STEP 1:	24 - 40 hours	$ 3,600 - $ 6,000
STEP 2:	8 - 16 hours	$ 1,200 - $ 2,400
STEP 3*a:	72 hours	$10,800
b:	54 hours	$ 8,100

    * Step 3 has been estimated using the following basis.

    (a)   4 hrs X 6 groups X 3 months
    (b)   3 hrs X 6 groups X 3 quarters

All consultant out-of-pocket expenses, e.g. travel accommodations, etc. and project-related expenses, such as manual/report/graphics production and computer processing will be additional and charged at cost or normal labor rate.

SORE BACKS Medical Center will receive an invoice each month for the work and expenses incurred the previous month. Payment is due upon receipt of the invoice.

If at any time you find it necessary or desirable to terminate the services of ABC Consulting, Inc., you are free to do so and are only obligated to pay our fees and expenses up to that point.

CONDITIONS OF ACCEPTANCE

The above fees will remain valid for a period of ninety days operative from the date of this

FIGURE 7.2.   (Continued.)

Mr. Mark Image
SORE BACKS Medical Center
July 14, 199X

Page 4

proposal. Should confirmation of acceptance be received after expiry of this ninety day period, we reserve the right to review and amend the quoted fees, in light of your circumstances and our current scale of fees.

Mark, I will call you next week to see where we go from here. I trust all is well at SORE BACKS and that you and the executive team continue to move forward.

Sincerely,

Andrea W. Needham

FIGURE 7.2.   (Continued.)

For Immediate Release   For Further Information
                                             (your name) (telephone #)

**FREE HOTEL SALES
TRAINING SESSION SET**

(City) (Date)--"How hotels can increase sales," is the title of a free, 90-minute seminar scheduled for (date) at (place), and designed to help hotel sales departments improve productivity.

The session, which will cover techniques ranging from cold-calling to generating additional business from current clients, is being sponsored by (name of firm).

(Optional paragraph) The (name of firm) was recently honored with the (name of award or any other kind of recognition), and has trained more than (number) of salespeople for more than (number of hotels).

A portion of the seminar will also focus on some new, innovative sales techniques, and will be given by (names), four of the top trainers in the industry.

Advance registration is required, and can be obtained by calling (number) between (hours).

####

FIGURE 7.3. News release targeted to local newspapers and trade journals in the hospitality industry.

For Immediate Release   For Further Information
                                             (your name) (telephone #)

HOW TO GET FREE PUBLICITY
SESSION SET FOR (DATE)

(City) (Date)--"How to Get Free Publicity," an hour-long seminar that details

exactly how businesses can obtain free media exposure, is the title of a special

(date) session scheduled to be held by the (name of city) chamber of Commerce

at its offices, (address).

(Name of consultant), a 10-year-veteran of the advertising and public relations

field, will be the speaker for the event, which is part of the chamber's program

to help local business improve sales.

Among the topics covered will be what kind of news the media wants, how to

approach the media, how to structure news releases, and the opportunities for

free television exposure.

(Name of consultant) will also detail how you use positive free publicity to

merchandise your business, and develop new customers. (Optional) (Name of

consultant) has been a communications practitioner in (name of city) since

(year), and has represented a variety of clients in industries ranging from

(names). (Name of consultant) is the recipient of (name of awards, honors or

noteworthy campaigns that were conducted).

For information on registration call (number), the (name of city) Chamber.

                            ###

FIGURE 7.4. News release targeted to the business community advertising a
Chamber-sponsored seminar.

MICHAEL DANIELS, PUBLISHERS
B O O K   N E W S

FOR IMMEDIATE RELEASE   CONTACT: Anita Horn
                                                                          310-838-4437

GETTING FAST, AUTHORITATIVE ANSWERS TO
EVERY HUMAN RESOURCE MANAGEMENT QUESTION

Companies heading toward the new millennium must comply with rapidly changing laws, re-engineer their organizations on the fly, and apply the latest research findings to improve quality and performance — without wasting time, money and energy. *Stern's SourceFinder®* helps make this possible. (Michael Daniels, revised and expanded, January 2, 1994, 482 pages).

Stern's, the *only* current, comprehensive, fully annotated directory to human resource management (HRM) information, provides fast access to over 3,800 information sources (books, periodicals, surveys, reports, databases, associations, etc.) – covering more than 8,000 HRM topics. Subdivided into 46 well-organized HRM specializations (Law, Compensation, HRIS, Training, Organization Development, etc.), *Stern's* makes the hunt for current, reliable information easy. Every entry contains a one-paragraph description and complete ordering information (name, address, phone, fax, price, pub. date, etc.).

This fully-revised and greatly-expanded 1994/1995 edition contains 1,100 more entries, 2,000 more topics and 7 more chapters than the preceding edition. Forty-five percent of the book is completely new. The remaining fifty-five percent has been thoroughly updated. The meticulously cross-referenced subject index has been enriched to reflect the very latest HRM concepts, terms and acronyms. And the author and title indexes and users' guide have been streamlined for even greater ease-of-use.

Dedicated to keeping registered *SourceFinder* users abreast of the latest information, *Stern's* has added a **FREE telephone update service**. Additionally, users receive a **FREE** (reg. $24.00) **one-year subscription to** *Stern's HR Management Review*, a quarterly newsletter featuring in-depth book reviews and editorials on cutting-edge HR and general management issues.

continued...

FIGURE 7.5.   News release targeted to human resource journals.

Introduced in 1991, as an extension of Stern & Associate's proprietary management consulting database service, **Stern's** quickly found its way to executive suites, corporate information centers and business libraries throughout the world — making it the premiere international guide to human resource management information. Users praise it for its content, scope and ease-of-use.

"What with downsizing and slashed consulting budgets, I can't rely on someone else to answer my HR questions. No one can know everything. But, with the **SourceFinder**, I can certainly find the things I need to know very quickly. Not a day goes by that I don't look something up in **Stern's**!"

Cleve Adams, Director, HR Management Transitions, Valley Presbyterian Hospital

"Building an HR department in the fast-paced environment of a newly-acquired national service company is a tough task. The **SourceFinder** helps me do my job by giving me fast access to the materials, organizations and experts we need. It's a beautifully organized book... so easy to use. I've even used the table of contents and the index to develop job titles and specifications! My copy is on my desk at all times. It's powerful!"

Bill Adair, Senior Vice President, Human Resources, Strategic Mortgage Services

◆

Title:	**Stern's SourceFinder®: Human Resource Management**
Authors:	Gerry Stern and Yvette Borcia
Pub. Date:	January 2, 1994
Price:	$169.95 (Paperback, 482 pages, indexes)
ISBN:	1-879162-20-2
To order call:	(310) 838-4437
or write:	Michael Daniels, Publishers
	P.O. Box 3233
	Culver City, CA 90231-3233

Limited review copies are available to qualified editorial requests.

MICHAEL DANIELS, PUBLISHERS

Publicity Department
11260 Overland Avenue, Suite 16A
Culver City, CA 90230
Tel (310) 838-4437 • Fax (310) 838-2344

FIGURE 7.5.   (Continued.)

<u>**For Immediate Release**</u>   For Further Information
                                        (your name) (telephone #)

<u>**(Name of Consultant) Launches**</u>
EXECUTIVE SEARCH FIRM

(City) (Date)--(Name of consultant), a 20-year veteran of the executive search industry, has opened offices, and will specialize in finding key executives for companies in the (name of industry).

(Name of consultant), who was recipient of (name award, honor, etc.), entered the executive search field in (year) with company. For the next (number of years) he concentrated on finding executives in the (name of industry). In (year) he left (name of company), and joined (name of company) where he was (title) for (number of years) before opening his own offices.

A graduate of (university) in (degree), (name of consultant) says "the industry has gone through some radical changes during the past few years, and our firm has developed a new innovative plan designed to attract top executives at a far lower cost than companies traditional spend."

(name of consultant) is located at (address). His/her telephone number is (number).

###

FIGURE 7.6.   News release targeted to local media as well as trade press.

RUDOLPH DEW & ASSOCIATES
CUSTOMIZED
OUTPLACEMENT SYSTEMS

**RUDOLPH DEW AND ASSOCIATES
CAREER CONSULTANTS INTRODUCES
A NEW GENERATION OF OUTPLACEMENT TECHNOLOGY
WHICH MAKES ALL PREVIOUS APPROACHES...
OBSOLETE**

FIGURE 7.7.   Consultant's brochure.

The New "Best Fit"™ System of Outplacement

A Five-Step Process to Help the Candidate Find a Better Job Faster and Often With More Compensation...

The Rudolph Dew & Associates' approach to outplacement is a systematic approach designed to help a job candidate:

- Look for new employment in the right places;
- Distinguish himself or herself from the competition for the particular job; and
- Negotiate a more favorable compensation package.

"Best Fit"™ outplacement technology grew out of experience, data bases, and tools gained from 45 years of human resources consulting by the Hay Group's interconnected network of 80 offices in 25 countries serving over 6000 companies.

Hay has done extensive consulting in the areas of management continuity and succession planning, organizational design, job design and evaluation, and organizational culture. Rudolph Dew & Associates has applied these experiences to the process of outplacement, and has enhanced them with several special features:

- **Company and Job Fit.** The greatest difficulty in finding a job lies in identifying the 15-20 percent of potential situations where the candidates will best fit. The "Best Fit"™ system identifies key fit-related factors for both candidate and company and provides data to help the candidate identify organizations which offer the best fit.

- **A Systematic Approach.** Our system has codified Hay's data bases and experience into a packaged, yet customized, system. As a result, Rudolph Dew & Associates reduces the customary dependence on the outplacement counselor, and provides consistency in the counseling process. Rather than a sole informational resource, our consultant now functions as a skilled leader through the process of the job fit.

- **A Solid Understanding of the Candidate's Worth.** Rudolph Dew & Associates' vast informational resources help the candidate better judge what he or she is worth in the job marketplace. We also help the candidate negotiate the best employment package possible.

The "Best Fit"™ Outplacement Technology

	Company Types		
	A	B	C
Business Fit		▨	
Management Fit			▨

1.   Determining the Best Fit

The key to our system is finding the type of job and company that is best suited to the individual's skills and personality. The typical candidate will fit into only 15-20 percent of the job opportunities available. We help the candidate target his or her search accordingly which results in less wasted time, better job offers, and less rejection/depression.

First, we make a business-oriented assessment of the candidate. Lengthy interviews are conducted with the candidate. Business-oriented psychological tests are also conducted. Data obtained is then assimilated into a detailed profile of the candidate, including the candidate's strengths in the following areas:

Company Fit
- Strategy
- Structure
- People Profile
- Managerial Systems
- Culture/Climate

Job Fit
- Team Building Skills
- Managerial Ability
- Ability to Work with Others
- Problem Solving
- Effectiveness and Impact
- Leadership

FIGURE 7.7.   (Continued.)

Like people, organizations are different. Differing business situations require different environments and ways of organizing, staffing, and managing. An organization's profile is determined by its external environment (i.e. life cycle, market approach, strategic challenge), and its internal environment (i.e. investment profile, goals, and approach set by top management).

Through its varied experience, the Hay Group determined that organizations fall into one of three broad profiles:

- **A.** Developing and Entrepreneurial Organizations
- **B.** Growing and Professional Organizations
- **C.** Mature and Administrative Organizations.

Our revolutionary approach to outplacement is based upon matching the candidate to the appropriate organization type.

Candidate Profile For	
Accomplishments	
Skills	
Qualifications	
Best Fit	

2.   Packaging the Candidate

Once the best company and job fit is determined, Rudolph Dew & Associates works to "package" the candidate to help him or her during the hiring decision. This packaging is done to organize the candidate's skills and qualifications into the framework most often used by the interviewer.

In this hard-hitting business world, there is no substitute for a candidate clearly knowing what he or she has to offer. Only when the candidate can differentiate himself or herself based upon accomplishment, managerial, and technological knowledge, can an effective interview take place.

3.   Preparing the Candidate for Marketing

Packaging the candidate is only part of Rudolph Dew & Associates' marketing-oriented approach to outplacement. Candidates are trained in how to differentiate themselves from the competition.

Candidates are trained in communications skills and equipped with the tools to better market themselves. For example, candidates receive customized:

- Guidelines for initial telephone conversations designed to help gain interviews;
- A 90-second drill to help first interviews get started on the right foot;
- A series of key messages to make an impression on the interviewer within the first few minutes;
- Advice on answering the 10 most important questions most commonly asked during interviews;
- Interview training utilizing videotaped simulations; and
- An interviewer-oriented resume.

The candidate also will benefit from our unique strength of being able to equip him or her to discuss with an interviewer the major issues facing the industry in which the hiring company operates.

Even more importantly, candidates gain the benefit of a unique sales training program developed by us based upon the experience of Hay's sales and marketing consulting group. Candidates are taught value-added consultative selling which helps them impress upon an interviewer the economic value they can bring to a firm.

FIGURE 7.7.   (Continued.)

4.   Conducting an Aggressive Sales Campaign

Finding a job is like fishing: you have to know the "hot" spots in which to look. Because its fit analysis categorizes the type of company and job for which the candidate is best suited, we can help conduct a highly targeted and focused job search campaign.

Using sophisticated data bases and fit analysis, we have changed the industry's standard approach of blindly and randomly searching for a job.

And with Rudolph Dew & Associates' professionally-targeted marketing/networking campaign, the candidate will spend less time looking for a job and be more able to concentrate on those positions that offer the greatest opportunity. In addition, our post interview review sessions are conducted in terms of business fit which helps further refine the job search.

5.   Improving the Candidate's Negotiating Position

Finally, our access to assessment and compensation data will help the candidate know the size of job he or she is most qualified for, and how much typical companies pay for similar jobs. This knowledge will strengthen the candidate's negotiating position.

But more importantly, Rudolph Dew & Associates' "value added" approach changes the candidate's negotiating posture from defensive to offensive. By being able to place a dollar value on what he or she can bring to a company, the candidate will be able to negotiate a better package of compensation and benefits.

Summary

The "Best Fit"™ system of customized outplacement provides a system and data bases unavailable elsewhere. By combining the experience, technology, and information developed from 45 years of the Hay Group's leading edge human resources consulting, we provide an added dimension to outplacement:

- Technology to identify the candidate's best fit.
- Teach the candidate to think in the terms of the hiring company.
- A codified and systematic process which reduces the dependency on the counselor as the primary source of technical knowledge.
- A highly customized approach which best packages the candidate.
- Training the candidate in differentiating himself or herself through adding value on the job.
- A second-to-none negotiations package.

Rudolph Dew & Associates
19401 South Vermont Ave.
Suite A-100
Torrance, CA 90502
(310) 323-7292

Tustin
(714) 669-0364

Woodland Hills
(818) 712-0581

Honolulu
(808) 528-4321

Phoenix
(602) 395-5765

FIGURE 7.7.   (Continued.)

About Stern & Associates

Compensation

We work with clients in designing achievement-based, total compensation programs that link the organization's business strategy and planning to all elements of the reward system, including: base salary, short- and long-term cash incentives, stock-based incentive plans, award and recognition systems, benefits, and perquisites. Areas of specialization include: sales incentive plans, executive and board of directors compensation, customized job/skill-based evaluation plans, and group and organization-wide incentive plans. Additionally, we conduct customized compensation and benefits surveys.

Organization

We identify and analyze organizational issues, and develop strategies and programs for achieving organizational effectiveness. We focus on such areas as: strategy and organization design, structure, job design, planning and decision making, control and coordination, team-work, communication, leadership and management, staffing levels, motivation, reward systems, culture, and employee attitudes. The design of compensation plans and conducting customer surveys may be involved in these studies.

Performance Management

We design performance management and appraisal systems which can integrate performance goal-setting, staffing, succession planning, career pathing, coaching, management development and training, and compensation.

Employee/Management Surveys

Our surveys provide a means of discovering organizational issues, measuring employee attitudes and motivation and identifying specific employee development and human resources needs. We design targeted questionnaires, conduct interviews, facilitate focus groups, develop action-oriented feedback processes, and assist management in translating findings into action plans and programs.

Communication

We asses our clients' communications patterns (formal and informal, written and oral, upward, downward, lateral, and external) and help them to formulate their communication goals and strengthen channels of communication. We also develop communication materials, including: policy manuals, employee handbooks, employee newsletters, and management presentations.

Research

Utilizing our proprietary database and other information resources, we are always available to assist our clients with their special information needs in all areas of human resource management.

Publications

- *Stern's SourceFinder®: Human Resource Management*
- *Stern's HR Management Review*

FIGURE 7.8.   "Resume"-type letter as alternative to brochure.

Gerry Stern consults in organization design and development, compensation, and human resource management. Areas of specialization include: individual, group and company-wide incentive plans; salary administration; performance management systems; organizational analysis, design and change; organizational and employee surveys; and the development of human resource management goals, strategy, function, and policy.

Gerry has provided consulting services to over 300 corporations, nationwide, in such sectors/ industries as: manufacturing (high technology, petroleum, food, pharmaceuticals, transportation, farming and earth-moving heavy equipment), service (health care, financial services, retailing and wholesaling, education, utilities), city and state government, consulting, and research.

Gerry holds a Master of Arts Degree in Labor and Industrial Relations from the Institute for Labor and Industrial Relations, University of Illinois and earned his Bachelor of Arts Degree in Economics from the State University of New York.

In addition to twenty years of consulting experience with Ernst & Young, Hewitt Associates, Peat Marwick, and Stern & Associates, Gerry spent seven years as a member of management in two Fortune 500 corporations, serving as director, employee relations, compensation and organization planning. He also served as an instructor in sales compensation for the American Compensation Association, and currently teaches "Motivation and Performance Management" at California State University, Northridge.

Together with his partner, Yvette Borcia, Gerry has authored *Stern's SourceFinder®: Human Resource Management*, a fully annotated information directory, and is co-editor of *Stern's HR Management Review*, a quarterly periodical on new publications in human resources, organization and general management.

He has made numerous presentations to professional and business associations, including the American Compensation Association, Group Health Association of America, Healthcare Human Resource Management Association, American Association of Advertising Agencies, the OD Network, the HR Roundtable, Southern California Personnel Technical Committee, Professionals in Human Resources Association and others.

Gerry's professional memberships include: the Society for Human Resource Management, American Compensation Association, Society for Industrial and Organizational Psychology, the Association for the Management of Organization Design, and the American Psychological Association. He is the founding director and current president of the Los Angeles Roundtable for the Analysis and Design of Organization.

FIGURE 7.9. Descriptive narrative focusing on consultant.

Yvette Borcia consults in organizational design and development, compensation, communication and human resource management.

In compensation, Yvette specializes in plan design, implementation and communication. She works with clients in such areas as: customized labor market surveys, sales and marketing incentive compensation, group/team incentives, managerial and executive *total* compensation, board of directors remuneration, job evaluation (market-, compensable factor-, and competency-based approaches), and benefits.

She also provides consulting services to clients in the areas of organization analysis, design development and structure, performance appraisal, employee surveys, customer satisfaction surveys, facilitation of problem-solving sessions, strategic planning and environmental scanning.

Yvette has expertise in interpersonal and mass communication, as well as small group dynamics, public address and graphic arts. She has developed a broad range of communication products, including: corporate policy manuals and handbooks, presentations, newsletters and special employee communication materials.

Yvette earned her Bachelor of Arts degree in Speech/Communication, with high honors, from the University of Illinois. Additionally, she earned her Professional Designation in Human Resources and Organization Development from the University of California, Los Angeles.

Prior to Founding Stern & Associates with Gerry Stern in 1985, Yvette served clients in business administration, education, personal management, theatrical production, communication and design. She retains ownership of Inklings, a graphic design and communication firm, established in 1980.

Yvette is co-author of *Stern's SourceFinder®: Human Resource Management* and co-editor of *Stern's HR Management Review*. She is a frequent speaker at professional and business association meetings, conferences and seminars, and teaches "Management and Leadership Communication" and "Professional Presentations" at California State University, Northridge.

Yvette's memberships include: Society for Human Resource Management, American Society for Training and Development, Association for the Management of Organization Design, and the International Association of Business Communicators. She is the founding co-director of the Los Angeles Roundtable for the Analysis and Design of Organization. Her pro-bono work has included co-founding the Screen Actors Guild's Children's Committee, where she was instrumental in drafting legislation to protect minors in the entertainment industry. Yvette is Vice Chair of Culver City's Civil Service Commission.

FIGURE 7.9.   (Continued.)

ORGANIZATIONS WE HAVE SERVED

Affiliated Hospitals of San Francisco
American Association of Advertising Agencies
American Building Systems, Inc.
American Isuzu Motors, Inc.
Ameron, Inc.
Anchor Savings and Loan Association
Automobile Clubof Southern California
Avco Financial Services, Inc.
Bakersfield Memorial Hospital
Bank of California
Beneficial Standard Life Insurance Company
Best Western, International
Black & Decker Corporation
Blue Cross of California
Bugle Boy
CALAVO (California Avacado Growers Assn.
California Assn. of Hospitals & Health Services
California Student Loan Finance Corporation
Childrens Hospital of Los Angeles
City of Indianapolis, Indiana
City of Palmer (Alaska)
Clark Equipment Company
Coca-Cola Bottling Company of Chicago
Control Data Corporation
Dart-Kraft, Inc.
Dart-Kraft, Styro Products Division
Dart-Karft, Tupperware International
Dodge Manufacturing Corporation
Electrical Power Research Institute (Palo Alto)
First Consulting Group
First Interstate Bankcorp
Fleetwood Industries, Inc.
Fluid Recycling Service, Inc.
Frank Holton & Company
Frito-Lay, Inc.
Frontier Oil & Gas Company
Fruehauf Corporation
General Group International
G. Heileman Brewing Company, Inc.
Greater Los Angeles Zoo Association
Griffin Financial Services, Inc.
Health Net
Holdrege Chamber of Commerce, Inc. (NE)
Home Savings of America (H. F. Alhmanson)
Hospital Council of Southern California
Hughes Helicopter
Information International, Inc.
IOLAB (Johnson & Johnson)
Iowa Beef Processors, Inc.
Jantzen, Inc.
Jewel Food Stores (National Tea)
Joliard
Joslyn Corporation
Jostens, Inc.
Katz & Associates
Lawry's Foods, Inc. (Lipton)

Lear Siegler Industries, Signal Division
Leucadia Water & Sanitation District
Little Company of Mary (Los Angeles)
Lugens Steel, Inc.
Manpower, Inc.
Market Compilation Research Bureau
Marsh Supermarkets
Massey-Ferguson, Inc.
Moody's Bible Institute
Moore Architectural Design
Mueller Pasta Company
Nabisco Specialty Foods Division
National Health Enhancement Systems
Nebraska State Department of Highways
Needham Harper Steers
Northrop Corporation
Optical Disc Corporation
PacifiCare Health Systems
Pacific Refining Company
Panke Machinery Corporation
PepsiCo American Building Systems, Inc.
Professional Budget Plan, Inc.
Quotron
Rexall Pharmaceuticals
Rexcel, Inc.
Rio Hondo Junior College
Ross Loos Hospital (Los Angeles)
Saga Foods, Inc.
Salt River Project (Arizona)
San Diego Transit Corporation
Santa Barbara Cottage Hospital
Schlumberger
Sentry Insurance
Sisters of Mercy Hospital (Idaho)
St. Francis Medical Center (Lynwood)
St. Lukes Hospital (Los Angeles)
State of Illinois, Department of Personnel
Strategic Mortgage Services
Summa Corp.
Tetra Tech, Inc.
Thatcher Glass
The Transition Group
The Walker Group
Tonka Toys, Inc.
Tosco Corporation
Toshiba America, Inc.
TRW Electronics Component
TRW Information Services
Twentieth Century Fox
U & I Sugar Company
Ultramar Ltd.
Union Bank (Los Angeles)
Varian
Western Gear Corperation
Wheelerbrator-Frye Corporation
Wick Building Systems, Inc.
Zellerbach Paper Company

Stern & Associates

FIGURE 7.10.   List of clients consultant has served.

RUDOLPH DEW & ASSOCIATES
OUTPLACEMENT AND CAREER COUNSELING
EXECUTIVE ASSESSMENT

RUDOLPH A. DEW
PRESIDENT

Rudy Dew has more than 34 years of Line Management and Corporate Human Resource experience.

In 1988, Rudy acquired the Western United States portion of Hay Career Consultants where he was their Regional Vice President for over six years. Before joining Hay Career Consultants, Rudy was Director of Personnel Development for the VSI Corporation, an international conglomerate of manufacturing and distribution companies headquartered in Pasadena, California. The VSI conglomerate included Voi-Shan - Aerospace Fasteners Manufacture, Cardkey Security Access Systems and Manufacturer, VSI Hardware and Fasteners, Greer Hydraulics - a fluid energy control company, Natter Manufacturing - sheet metal design and fabrication, and the DME Company - plastic tool and die manufacture and supplies. VSI had facilities at 98 locations in 19 states with 30 of these located on the West Coast.

While at VSI Rudy designed, established and implemented technical, supervisory and executive development programs for all company locations. His responsibilities also included the executive succession program and the development and administration of a video based mass communication system which linked all company locations.

Previously, Rudy was employed at Southern California Edison, where he held both line and staff responsibilities over a 20 year period. While there he held the positions of Senior Sales Representative, Distribution Engineer, Area Manager, Corporate Employment Manager, and finally Corporate Manager of Organizational and Employee Development. In the latter position he and his staff designed, developed, and administered career programs, assessment centers and training programs for the 14,000 employees employed by Southern California Edison.

Rudy received his B.S. degree in Economics from the University of Redlands and a MBA degree with a major in Organizational Development from the University of Southern California. He has completed additional work at UCLA, University of Wisconsin and Stanford University. As Adjunct Instructor, he has over the past 11 years taught courses in Small Business Administration, EEO, and HRS functions at the Mount San Antonio College in Walnut, California. He has also been a guest lecturer at Princeton University, Brigham Young University, and the University of Southern California Doctoral Program. He has served on five college advisory boards (USC Business School, California State University of Northridge, Cerritos College, Mount San Antonio College and Pasadena City College).

Rudy has conducted numerous speaking engagements for both local and national personnel and industrial relations directors associations. He is listed in Who's Who in California and Who's Who in the West.

19401 S. Vermont Avenue, Suite A-100, Torrance, CA 90501 - (310) 323-7292

Woodland Hills, CA - (818) 712-0581   Tustin, CA - (714) 669-0364   Honolulu, HI - (808) 528-4321   Phoenix, AZ - (602) 277-1545

FIGURE 7.11.   Descriptive narrative focusing on consultant and clients served.

RUDOLPH DEW & ASSOCIATES
OUTPLACEMENT AND CAREER COUNSELING
EXECUTIVE ASSESSMENT

RUDOLPH DEW & ASSOCIATES
PROFESSIONAL STAFF

RUDOLPH A. DEW, PRESIDENT   In 1988, Rudy Dew acquired the Western United States portion of Hay Career Consultants where he was their Regional Vice President for over six years. Before joining Hay, Rudy had been with VSI Corporation and had over 34 years experience with Southern California Edison. During that time Rudy held positions as Director of Personnel Development, Senior Sales Representative, Distribution Engineer, Area Manager, Corporate Employment Manager and Manager of Organizational and Employee Development. Rudy received his B.S. degree in Economics and an M.B.A. with a major in Organizational Development from USC. As an Adjunct Instructor he has taught courses in Small Business Administration, EEO and HRS functions. He has also been a guest lecturer at Princeton University, Brigham Young University and the University of Southern California Doctoral Program. He has served on five college advisory boards.

PHILIP R. GARR, SENIOR VICE PRESIDENT   Phil Garr has over 28 years of outplacement and communications industry experience in Human Resources, Marketing, Operations and Comptrollers. He has diverse experience in Line Management and Corporate Staff at Pacific Bell and AT&T. Prior to joining Dew & Associates in 1988, he was Director of Human Resources responsible for Management Employment and Development, and Training at Pacific Bell. Phil has a B.A. degree in Economics from the University of Washington and a M.S. in Management from Pace University in New York.

AMY E. CISCO, VICE PRESIDENT   Amy Cisco has over 17 years progressive management, human resources, training and program development experience in the health care, insurance and government fields. Amy has been associated with Straub Clinic & Hospital, City of Honolulu, and Hawaii Medical Service Association, the Blue Cross Blue Shield Plan for Hawaii. She has held positions of Director of Employee Relations and Benefits, Equal Opportunity Officer and Management Analyst. Amy received her Bachelors Degree in Sociology and Masters Degree in Public Administration from USC.

ROBERT N. GOLD, VICE PRESIDENT   Bob Gold has been a Management Consultant since 1983 specializing in strategic planning, marketing and organizational development for companies in transition. He was with Arthur D. Little, Inc., Theodore Barry & Associates and headed his own consulting firm. Previously, Bob spent five years with First Interstate Bank of California in staff positions ranging from Public Policy Planning to Area Financial Controller. His B.A. and M.A. degrees are in Philosophy and he has a M.B.A. in Strategic Planning from UCLA.

DAVID P. MCGOWAN, VICE PRESIDENT   Dave McGowan has nearly 30 years of experience in Human Resources, Administration, MIS and Sales within the high technology, manufacturing, communications and executive recruiting industries. Dave has been associated with Honeywell, GTE, LTX, and most recently, Personnel Resource Corporation. Dave has a B.A. in English from Yale University. In the early 1970's, while at Honeywell, he established and operated their first Internal Outplacement Program.

JAMES A. SHERIDAN, VICE PRESIDENT   Jim Sheridan joined Rudolph Dew & Associates after a career in corporate management at AT&T and the management consulting firms of Towers Perrin Forster & Crosby (TPF&C), Cresap McCormick and Padget (CMP), Moran Stahl & Boyer (MS&B) and EuroCal Consultants. With 28 years in technical and managerial experience with Fortune 500 companies, he brings a diversity of knowledge to Dew & Associates. Jim has a B.A. and M.A. from University of Kansas at Wichita. A founding member of the Human Resource Planning Society, Jim is recognized as an expert in human resource forecasting and planning. He has lectured and taught at New York University, Cornell, and Columbia among others. As an inventor, two U.S. patents have been issued in his name.

TINA WONG, VICE PRESIDENT TRAINING & GROUP SERVICES   Tina Wong has over 10 years experience in Human Resources training and development, instructional design and outplacement within Corporate, Subsidiary and Consulting arenas. Tina was with Hay Career Consultants, VSI Corporation and on staff at the University of Southern California School of Business/Experiential Learning Center. Tina has conducted career workshops and post workshop counseling, implemented and conducted management/supervisory training programs, and coordinated a video based telecommunication network. Tina has a Bachelor's and a Master's degree in Education and a Master's degree in Instructional Technology from University of Southern California.   19401 S. Vermont Avenue, Suite A-100, Torrance, CA 90501 - (310) 323-7292

Woodland Hills, CA - (818) 712-0581   Tustin, CA - (714) 669-0364   Honolulu, HI - (808) 528-4321   Phoenix, AZ - (602) 277-1545

FIGURE 7.12.   Descriptive narrative of consultant's associates.

PROFESSIONAL STAFF

GEORGE M. DeLONG, Ph.D   Dr. George DeLong, a psychologist certified by the Arizona Board of Psychologist Examiners, has over 13 years in private practice as President and General Manager of Behavioral Health Systems, Inc. His areas of specialization include diagnostic psychological examination, with emphasis on vocational evaluation. Dr. DeLong has a B.A. in Psychology, and a M.A. and Ph.D. from the clinical psychology training program at Arizona State University.

DAVID SCULLY, CONSULTANT   David Scully has over 25 years of business, academic and government experience. Prior to joining Rudolph Dew & Associates, David spent over two years as an adjunct professor at National University. Teaching graduate courses in Information Management Systems and Career Development. For the previous fourteen years, he was manager of Customer and Internal Training with ACDAM INC, a high-tech computer graphics company with responsibility for the international training group. David has a M.S. Degree and a Doctorate of Education Degree, both in Instructional Design from the University of Southern California.

ALAN S. LERT, Ph.D.   Dr. Alan Lert is a licensed psychologist in California, New Jersey and Pennsylvania and has maintained a private practice in Southern California for over 10 years. He specializes in psychological assessment and evaluation, and counseling. He received his B.A. degree in Psychology from Northwestern University and both his M.A. and Ph.D. degrees in psychology from the University of Southern California.

MARGARITA BORDA, CONSULTANT   Margarita has over 11 years in career planning and counseling, including outplacement services to businesses in transition and in multi-cultural diversity training. She has held instructor and counselor positions at various community colleges, including Long Beach City College. Margarita speaks fluent Spanish. She holds as a B.A. degree in Psychology and a M.S. degree in Counseling Psychology.

HANK FELDMANN, CONSULTANT   Hank Feldmann has over 27 years of experience as both a line manager and a consultant. His background includes managing his own consulting firm and being a Principal Consultant managing compensation and organization planning with a Big Six Accounting firm. He has also held positions with Fortune 500 corporations as an Employment Interviewer, Wage and Salary Analyst, Labor Relations Advisor and Director of Employee Relations. He was the General Manager of Personnel for a government aerospace agency. Hank received his B.A. in Economics and has earned an M.B.A. He is also an Accredited Personnel Diplomate.

JODY MARTIN, CONSULTANT   Jody Martin has over 17 years experience in marketing, sales, market research, data processing, engineering, operations and project management. Jody has taught courses for UCLA Extension, Moorpark College, California Lutheran College and is on the advisory board of Moorpark College. She has a B.S. with a double major, Psychology/Kinesthiology.

SUSAN A. MURPHY, CONSULTANT   Susan Murphy has 24 years of experience with two Fortune 500 companies, acute care hospitals and a private consulting practice. Prior to her association with Rudolph Dew & Associates, she was a Vice President with American Medical International, Inc. She also served as the Director of Organization and Management Development where she was instrumental in developing the AMI Corporate College for Executive Leadership. Her B.A. in Nursing is from Vanderbilt University and she holds a M.B.A. from Pepperdine University.

MARTHA W. PHILLIPS, CONSULTANT   Martha Phillips has over 22 years experience in sales, marketing, human resources, training and development in a variety of industries. Martha has been Vice President and General Manager of Ergotech, Inc. and Director of Marketing Support for Lexitron Corporation. Martha has a B.A. with a double major in Psychology/Sociology.

JAMES F. SCOOLER, M.C., CONSULTANT   Jim Scooler has over 20 years experience in counseling and training. His experience includes being counseling supervisor and organization unit manager for Maricopa County, Arizona and teaching at the community college level. Jim has a B.A. degree in Psychology and a Master of Counseling degree.

19401 S. Vermont Avenue, Suite A-100, Torrance, CA 90501 - (310) 323-7292

Woodland Hills, CA - (818) 712-0581   Tustin, CA - (714) 669-0364   Honolulu, HI - (808) 528-4321   Phoenix, AZ - (602) 277-1545

FIGURE 7.12.   (Continued.)

7302 MARINA PACIFICA DRIVE SOUTH, KEY 12
LONG BEACH, CA 90803

SERVICES

Established in 1988, KMG Enterprises provides consulting services to
manufacturing and distribution companies in the areas of general management,
manufacturing and industrial engineering. Specifically:

- Audit and analysis; target in on where can profits be improved.
- Manufacturing strategy, plant location, **relocation**.
- Process and work flow analysis; plant **layout** (CAD).
- Quality audits, systems design, ISO 9000 & TQM.
- Cost reduction, methods, workers, tools and machinery.
- Paper systems design; make computer systems work effectively.
- Labor standards and **positive** incentives
- **Just-In-Time** systems, taught and installed;
  - $ improve quality significantly,
  - $ reduce rework and work in process,
  - $ drastically improve customer **lead time**,
  - $ reduce labor costs, improve **productivity**,
  - $ reduce inventories, release floor space

QUALIFICATIONS AND EXPERIENCE

K. Michael Green holds a BA in Business from Claremont McKenna College and a
BS and MS in Industrial Engineering from Stanford University and is a
Certified Management Consultant. He has designed, started up and operated
industrial engineering departments for major companies such as Honeywell,
General Tire and Wyandotte Chemicals (13 years). Moving from staff to
operations, he successfully turned around several smaller fully integrated
(product design, sales, manufacturing and accounting; P & L responsibility)
manufacturing and marketing companies as Vice President/General Manager
(16years).

Mr. Green has hands-on experience with a wide variety of industrial processes,
ranging from metal working, plastics, and rubber to electronics. As a
consultant, he has clients in a variety of machining processes, metal
fabrication and foundry, stamping, electronic assembly, non-destructive
testing, plastic film processing, precast cement products, glass printing,
stain glass assembly, manufactured housing, furniture manufacturing, specialty
lighting fixtures, rubber and plastic injection and compression molding,
carbonation devices, mail sorting and stuffing, orthopedic devices, resistance
welding machines, plastic and metal plating, specialty chemicals, wire cord
manufacture, among others.

K. Michael Green, MSIE, CMC
Certified Management Consultant

(310) 799-9316

FIGURE 7.13.   Consultant's qualifications and experience letter.

K. Michael Green, CMC
7302 Marina Pacifica Dr. So. Key 12
Long Beach, CA 90803
(310) 799 9316

Education

1956-1958   Stanford University - M.S. Industrial Engineering
                        B.S. Industrial Engineering

1953-1956   Claremont McKenna College - B.A. Business Administration

Employment History

1988-present   KMG Enterprises, Long Beach, Ca. - Principal
                        General management and industrial engineering consulting practice.

1984-1988   Fuqua Homes, Inc., Corona, Ca. - VP General Manager
                        factory housing - P & L, sales, production, product marketing and design.

1982-1983   Ormond Electronic Scales, Santa Fe Springs, Ca. - VP Gen. Mgr.
                        electronics - P & L, sales, production, new product design and development.

1976-1982   Guerdon Industries, Woodland, Oxnard, Marino, Ca. - VP Gen. Mgr.
                        factory housing - P & L, sales, production, marketing, product design.

1975-1976   International Screw Company, Mt. Clemens, Mi.(Microdot) - VP Gen. Mgr.
                        cold heading - P & L, production, product design, equipment acquisition.

1972-1974   Redman Industries, Honeybrook, Pa. - General Manager -
                        factory housing - P & L, sales, production, design, development and marketing.

1968-1972   BASF Wyandotte, Wyandotte, Mi. - Director of Industrial Engineering
                        chemicals - Projects in production, plant expansion and modification, maintenance
                        controls and analysis, plant design and various marketing projects.

1964-1968   Genco (General Tire & Rubber), Wabash, In. - Mgr. Ind. Eng., Asst. Plant Manager
                        rubber & plastics - Projects in production efficiency, capital justification, materials
                        handling, wage incentives, union negotiations. Rejuvenated IE dept.

1959-1964   Honeywell, Inc., Minneapolis, Mn.; Wabash, In. - Ind. Eng. and Chief Industrial Eng.
                        electro-mechanical devices - Projects in production, labor efficiency, plant layout,
                        material handling, computer and paperwork systems, value analysis teams and work
                        simplification teams. Designed and established new industrial engineering dept.

Professional Affiliations

Western Manufactured Housing Institute, Chairman Northern California
American Institute of Industrial Engineers; Past President, Vice President LA Chapter
Institute of Mananagement Consultants; Board of Directors, Certified Management Consultant (CMC)
Association of Professional Consultants; Board of Directors

FIGURE 7.13.   (Continued.)

RUDOLPH DEW & ASSOCIATES
OUTPLACEMENT AND CAREER COUNSELING
EXECUTIVE ASSESSMENT

TIME LIMITED PROGRAM WITH OFFICE SERVICES

Our services will include:

- A two-day career continuation workshop.
  - a.   Self marketing techniques
  - b.   Contact development
  - c.   Interview training
  - d.   Campaign design
  - e.   Negotiating the best offer

- Preparation and printing of a resume.

- Printing of stationery.

- Preparation of a reference statement.

- A mailing to 50 Executive Search firms from our computerized listing of over 4,000 companies.

- Up to 16 hours of counseling as needed within three months.

- Office support for three months: Office, typing, mailing, phones, answering service, etc.

- Access to our Hot Job Bank Listing of open jobs.

- Limited testing.

- Over 100 volume Resource Library providing information on companies, industries, etc., and computer access to over 10,000,000 company information files.

- Consultation on job selection and salary negotiations.

This program is not the same as our Individual Executive Program. For example, psychological testing and unlimited counseling are not included.

19401 S. Vermont Avenue, Suite A-100, Torrance, CA 90501 - (310) 323-7292

Woodland Hills, CA - (818) 712-0581   Tustin, CA - (714) 669-0891   Honolulu, HI - (808) 528-4321   Phoenix, AZ - (602) 277-1545

FIGURE 7.14.   Time limited program.

RUDOLPH DEW & ASSOCIATES
OUTPLACEMENT AND CAREER COUNSELING
EXECUTIVE ASSESSMENT

Two-Day Group Program

■ **FIRST DAY**

Orientation	Objective Setting	Resumes

• Why You Are Here
• Curriculum To Be Covered
• Who We Are
• Who You Are
• Personal Information Forms
• Areas of Concern
• Skills Inventory
• Personal Values
	• How Jobs Are Filled
	• Marketplace Realities
	• Marketing One's Self
	• Skills/Experience Transfer
	• Life Planning
	• Setting Objectives
	• Advice/Referral Methodology
	• Research Tools
		• Resume Objectives
		• Styles/Types
		• Quantifiable
		  Accomplishments
		• Design-Workshop
		  Assignments:
		  Resume
		  References
		  "Why I am Here"

■■ **SECOND DAY**

Individual Counseling	Interview Training	Campaign Design
One-on-one Sessions Within a Workshop: • Objectives Clarification • Resume Completion • Personal Strategies	• Build Your Potential • Interview Preparation • Do's and Don't's • Questions You May Be Asked • Questions You Should Ask • Interview Critique • Role Playing	• Campaign Strategy • Keeping Control: Use of Forms • Contact Development • Correspondence Preparation • Successful Telephone Use • Advertisements, Agencies • Salary Negotiations • Job Acceptance Procedures • Lifetime Networks

Program Time Analysis	Hours
Workshop (All Participants)	8
Supervised Work Programs (All Participants)	5
Individualized Counseling	1
TOTAL	**14**

© RUDOLPH DEW & ASSOCIATES 1988

19401 S. Vermont Avenue, Suite A-100, Torrance, CA 90501 - (310) 323-7292

Woodland Hills, CA - (818) 712-0581   Tustin, CA - (714) 669-0891   Honolulu, HI - (808) 528-4321   Phoenix, AZ - (602) 277-1545

FIGURE 7.14. (Continued.)

Time Limited Program

RUDOLPH DEW & ASSOCIATES
OUTPLACEMENT AND CAREER COUNSELING
EXECUTIVE ASSESSMENT

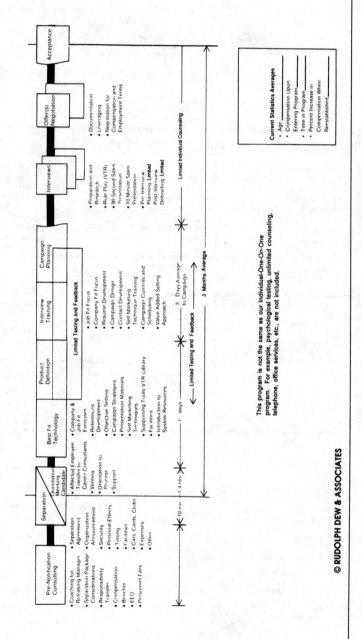

This program is not the same as our Individual-One-On-One program. For example, psychological testing, unlimited counseling, telephone, office services, etc., are not included.

© RUDOLPH DEW & ASSOCIATES

FIGURE 7.14. (Continued.)

RUDOLPH DEW & ASSOCIATES
OUTPLACEMENT AND CAREER COUNSELING
EXECUTIVE ASSESSMENT

INDIVIDUAL EXECUTIVE PROGRAM

This process is specifically tailored to the candidate in question.   Personalized career counseling services always include, but are not limited to:

- Initial and private consultation to assess and deal with prevailing attitudes and emotions, with emphasis on family and financial management.

- Vocational testing and assessment by a licensed management psychologist (8 Hours).

- Development of personal presentation materials.

- Securing company references.

- Instruction on the existing job market and various job changing systems.

- Interview and negotiation training with closed circuit television and videotape replay.

- Personally assigned career counselor.

- Development of appropriate marketing campaigns.

- Reproduction of resume and letterhead.

- Office support - office, phones, answering service, typing, postage, etc.

- On-going critique of campaign activity and interview results.

- Letters to executive search firms (local, national, international)
  - over 4,000 on our computer.

- Access to national and local compensation and benefit data bases.

- Access to our Hot Job Bank of open listings.

- Over 100 volume Resource Library providing information on companies, industries, etc. and computer access to over 10,000,000 company information files.

- Consultation on job selections and salary negotiations.

- Continued counseling following career decisions.

- Assistance on starting own business or purchasing a franchise (including writing a business plan, if appropriate).

19401 S. Vermont Avenue, Suite A-100, Torrance, CA 90501 - (310) 323-7292

Woodland Hills, CA - (818) 712-0581   Tustin, CA - (714) 669-0891   Honolulu, HI - (808) 528-4321   Phoenix, AZ - (602) 277-1545

FIGURE 7.15.   Individual executive program.

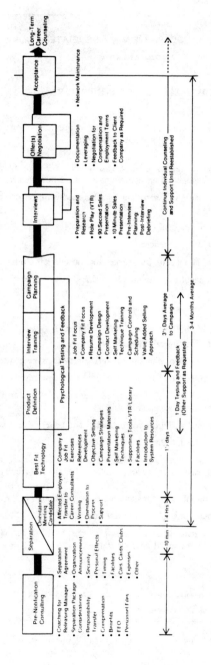

Individual Executive Program

FIGURE 7.15. (Continued.)

May 3, 199X

Ms. B. Emmett
Vice President, Human Resources
Woldwood HealthCare
1325 Codding Street
Woldwood, CA XXXXX

Dear Brigette:

As I understand it, you are seeking a consulting organization that provides a creative, possibly even "new age" twist to healthcare organizations and to human resources management within healthcare. Your needs include familiarity with healthcare care issues, a track record in innovation in human resources management within a service industry, a risk taker in identifying, recommending and developing new and different approaches to compensation and performance management, and an awareness of specific issues within union and nonunion environments.

BACKGROUND

ABC & Associates, Inc. (ABC) has been in business since 1984. I started the consulting practice after being with LARGE Associates in the United Kingdom and the USA. My preference in consulting is to work with service organizations and have gathered around me a team of consultants who also prefer the challenge of assisting service organizations, specifically healthcare, to not only survive but succeed in the nineties. ABC has become recognized for its work within healthcare. ABC also works successfully in the light industrial, high technology, food processing and utility industries.

Our preference for service organizations satisfies our individual and collective needs to be challenged by clients. There are few answers to management and human resources issues within service industries and those answers found tend to fit each situation very differently.

The service industry holds many unique characteristics. To be successful, a service company must allow the *customer* to "dictate" the organization structure, job design, and the performance-based compensation program. In healthcare, the difficulty has been in agreeing who the primary customer(s) is(are) and therefore, the indecision has lead to many internal management and human resource issues.

FIGURE 7.16. Follow-up letter.

Ms. B. Emmett
Woldwood HealthCare
May 3, 199X

Page 2

Because of the necessary focus on the customer, service organizations lend themselves very strongly to using employee design teams to develop and implement new human resources programs. The employee tends to be the individual with the most crucial contact with the customer. This enables the employee to better define the necessary organization relationships and success factors that need to become the underpinning of business success. While that is a benefit, I strongly suspect that the real key to success of employee design team that they help "buy in" of the final program. ms is the quality of customer knowledge of the front line employee.

SUCCESSFUL PROJECTS

Over the years we have had many success stories. A success story to us emphasizes the new and different that we are asked and permitted to do for an organization. The past three years have been interesting as even though the economy and minimal business success was demanding creativity, few clients have been able to take the leap of faith in their own judgement and change human resources philosophies dramatically.

Two clients have provided us with that challenge -- INNOVATIVE PsychHealth (IP) and WONDERFUL CO. (WC). In each case, the client agreed to an employee design team in developing a performance-based compensation program. The Design Teams each had managers, supervisors, and non-management employees.

In the case of IP, the Design team also recommended a new organization structure based solely on a team environment. After over 100 hours of collective deliberation and much more of individual deliberation, the Design Team felt that the best way to serve the customers -- patients, physicians, and third party payors -- was to adopt a team organization structure would be the most cost-effective.

In the case of WC, the Design Team, again with over 100 hours of deliberation, recommended the elimination of compensation entitlement based on tenure. This was a major and very dramatic change of direction for WC. 139 years of history had compensation practices well endowed with a cradle-to-grave entitlement mentality.

FIGURE 7.16. (Continued.)

Ms. B. Emmett
Woldwood HealthCare
May 3, 199X

Page 3

Our role in these two projects was facilitation. Each Design Team received minimal education by us on compensation. It is important in these scenarios that the consultants and compensation and human resources personnel do not "taint" the Design Team with old ideas and practices. I feel very strongly that organizations can not tackle something as large as a change in the performance management and compensation program using internal resources only. The key to the Design Team success is for each individual to feel "safe" and intellectually challenged. It is difficult or maybe impossible for an insider to provide that environment.

In addition, to these two projects we continue to work extensively with other healthcare providers and can submit references to you if you wish.

POSSIBLE APPROACH

It should be emphasized that at this stage it is impossible to predict the nature and type of project that Woldwood would need. However, you asked for an overview of an approach for developing a performance-based compensation program so I am outlining the typical steps we might adopt for an employee design team approach.

1)   Consultant Orientation

The consultants will meet with individuals and groups to learn more about the current internal climate of Woldwood . These meetings will provide a better understanding of the current operational, communication, problem-solving and decision-making processes. Each meeting will be between one to two hours in duration.

Issues found will be summarized and provided to the Vice President of Human Resources and the President and Chief Executive Officer.

2)   Development of the Performance Management and Compensation Program

The approach recommended for consideration by Woldwood is to use a Design Team. The ideal membership would be between 10 - 15 people and consist of managers and employees who represent different business areas and levels within Woldwood. It is

FIGURE 7.16.   (Continued.)

Ms. B. Emmett
Woldwood HealthCare
May 3, 199X

Page 4

regretted that bargaining unit personnel cannot participate on the Design Team. This action would be construed as direct dealing.

The Design Team will meet with the consultants for 2 - 3 days per week for about 6 - 8 weeks depending upon progress and results. The consultants role is to facilitate the Design Team. Initially, the consultants will introduce performance management and compensation concepts to the group and present options that have been successful. The Design Team will then work with the consultants to develop objectives, methodology, and implementation timeframe for the proposed program for Woldwood .

The recommended program may include task/outcome/role descriptions, base salary plan, incentive plan, success measures, award opportunities, proposed participants, and administrative guidelines.

As part of the implementation plan, a key task of the Design Team will be to develop an extensive communications plan. Ongoing communications will be necessary to introduce the new program, expedite the resolution of issues, and monitor the success of the plan.

3)   *Economic Modelling of the Proposed Compensation Program*

The economic modelling of the proposed compensation program will be carried out by the Human Resources Department at Woldwood or by ABC. The compensation program must be economically viable based on economic modeling under various business scenarios. Funding options will be included in the final presentations.

4)   *Refinement of the Performance Management and Compensation Program*

The compensation plan design and its implementation needs to be tested on potential recipients. At this stage of the planning process, it would appear that focus groups may form the most effective test groups. The Design Team will be asked to make recommendations regarding the most viable approach for presentation and discussion with the potential user population.

FIGURE 7.16.   (Continued.)

Ms. B. Emmett
Woldwood HealthCare
May 3, 199X

Page 5

> The Design Team will take the results of the testing process and refine the compensation program design, prepare a detailed implementation plan, and develop administrative policies and procedures.
>
> *5)   Development of Recommendations and an Implementation Plan*
>
> The consultants will take the results of the Design Team's work and develop a summary report containing the recommendations and costs for the proposed program. This will initially be presented to the Vice President of Human Resources. Upon review and agreement, the summary report will be presented to and discussed with the senior management team at Woldwood .

The next steps are obviously unknown at this point in time. They will be formulated and presented to the senior management group along with the proposed performance-based compensation program.

PROFESSIONAL FEES

Our professional fee structure consists of a usual charge for professional services of between $90.00 and $250.00 per hour depending upon the level and type of consultant used. This fee is charged only for the time we spend on a project and includes general administrative expenses, e.g. regular typing, regular mail and telephone calls.

All consultant out-of-pocket expenses, e.g. travel accommodations, etc. and project-related expenses, such as manual/report/graphics production and computer processing will be additional and charged to Woldwood at cost or normal labor rate.

Woldwood will receive an invoice each month for the work and expenses incurred the previous month. Payment is due upon receipt of the invoice.

If at any time you find it necessary or desirable to terminate the services of ABC, you are free to do so and are only obligated to pay our fees and expenses up to that point.

FIGURE 7.16.   (Continued.)

Ms. B. Emmett
Woldwood HealthCare
May 3, 199X

Page 6

Conditions of Acceptance

The above fees will remain valid for a period of six months operative from the date of this letter. Should confirmation of acceptance be received after expiry of this six month period, we reserve the right to review and amend the quoted fees, in light of your circumstances and our current scale of fees.

Information obtained in the assignment will be treated as entirely confidential by ABC. We would appreciate your cooperation in treating the information and techniques of ABC in a similar fashion as far as third parties are concerned.

SUMMARY

In summary, our expertise and interest lies in assisting progressive service organizations develop and implement human resources programs that reflect, reward and recognize the real needs of the "customer", whomever that may be. This requires both the consultants and senior management to take risks and needs full commitment from the client.

The information provided by you some months ago is not enough for me to estimate professional fees. Assuming that you would like to talk further with us, we will be happy to meet with you and discuss your needs in more depth. At that time, we will provide you with a firm professional fee estimate.

I look forward to meeting with you and possibly working with you. I believe the next step is to meet with you to finalize the project details so that we may provide fee estimates.

Sincerely,

Any. B. Consultant

FIGURE 7.16.   (Continued.)

FIGURE 7.17.   The "SourceFinder."

Free Newsletter

Your purchase of *Stern's SourceFinder*® entitles you to a FREE one-year subscription to **Stern's HR Management Review**, a quarterly newsletter of editorial opinion and in-depth reviews of new publications in organization, management and human resources. If you purchased *Stern's* directly from the publisher, your subscription will begin immediately. If you obtained your book from a book store, book-buying service or a catalog, your subscription will begin when you notify Michael Daniels, Publishers: P.O. Box 3233, Culver City, CA 90231-3233, (310) 838-4437.

Free Update Service

While this book has been fixed in time, our database is constantly changing. So, if a telephone number we list is no longer in service, or you can't find a listing for the latest HR innovation, just pick up a phone and call Stern & Associates at (310) 838-0551.

Beyond the SourceFinder

From time-to-time, you may need to go beyond the *SourceFinder* and confer with an expert, but do not require on-site consulting services. To meet those needs, we have introduced *tele-consulting*. Tele-consulting services include: answering technical questions, problem-solving, program development and creative brainstorming. You state your needs over the phone, or write to us, and we respond by phone, facsimile or mail. You pay nothing until you've approved our proposed approach and fee. It is simple, direct, and time- and cost-effective.

The Authors

Gerry Stern and Yvette Borcia are partners in Stern & Associates, a human resource management consulting firm specializing in strategy-based compensation and organization services. They are recognized for their interdisciplinary approach and innovative solutions to complex organizational issues. Their unique blend of perspectives and expertise helps clients achieve goals of quality, service, productivity and profitability.

Stern & Associates

Stern & Associates, an independent management consulting firm, was founded in 1985. The firm serves clients in all industry sectors, public and private, for-profit and not-for-profit, from Fortune 500 corporations to entrepreneurial start-ups. Stern & Associates is an affiliate of The Global Consortium, Inc., an international network of management consultants.

Past consulting assignments have included: individual, group and organization-wide incentive plans; job- and skill-based pay systems; integrated customer-focused studies of organization design, processes and culture; performance management programs; board-of-directors remuneration programs; executive search; employee surveys; employee communication programs; policy and procedures; total compensation programs; goal-setting, facilitation of group collaboration and change efforts, and development of organization analysis instruments and processes.

FIGURE 7.18. Benefits of purchasing the "SourceFinder."

User's Guide

FIVE STEPS:

EXAMPLE:

1 Define your problem.

```
┌─────────────── PROBLEM ───────────────┐
You're working your way up the HR ladder the
hard way – with a degree in musicology and a
lot of on-the-job experience. You know your
career would benefit from professional HR
accreditation, but you don't know who offers it
or how to study for the exam.
```

2 Select appropriate index.

There are **3 indexes**. For this problem,
the "subject index" is appropriate.

```
┌─────────────── INDEXES ───────────────┐
                        ┌─ Subject
                           Title
                           Author
```

**3 Choose key word(s)
in that index.**

```
┌──────── SUBJECT INDEX KEY WORDS ────────┐
"human resource management professionals"
            "accreditation"
          "training programs"
```

4 Locate reference number(s).

Find key word(s) in **bold print**.
Specific sub-topics are indented beneath
key word(s).

```
┌──────────── SUBJECT INDEX ────────────┐
compensation arrangements, 465
Accreditation
  (see also Human resource management professionals)
benefits, 73
human resource management
   competency assessment, 1393, 1394
   self-study, 1527
human resource professionals
   institute, 1428
   self-study program, 1420, 1538
organization development
   concept, 2764
```

REFERENCE
NUMBER

**5 Find your entry designated
by reference number(s).**

The indexes refer you to reference
numbers, *not page numbers*.
Reference numbers are listed in
numerical sequence.

	TITLE	ADDRESS	FAX
AUTHOR(S)	SOURCE	TELEPHONE	

1420 **HRCI Certification Study Guide**
Weinberg, Raymond B.; Mathis, Robert L; and
Cherrington, David J.

SHRM Distribution Center, 1600 West 82nd Street,
No. 200, Minneapolis, MN 55431, Tel: (800) 444-
5006 or (612) 885-5588, Fax: (612) 885-5569

*Self-study program. Helps the reader prepare for
Professional and Senior Professional accreditation in
Human Resources. Includes a 100-question
practice examination, bibliography and references.*
170 pp. Fully revised. 1993. SHRM members:
$15.00. Non-members: $20.00.

CATEGORY PAGES PRICE PUB. DATE COMMENTS

**CONTACT SOURCE
BEFORE ORDERING
TO CONFIRM PRICE
AND AVAILABILITY**

FIGURE 7.19.   A user's guide, showing detailed entries, aiding in the success of
the "SourceFinder."

Contents

❧

FIGURE 7.19.   (Continued.)

A

Absenteeism
(see also Turnover)
attendance improvement, 3428, 3453, 3470
tardiness and, 1674, 3427
turnover and
hiring and layoff trends, 3437
survey, 3436
Abstracts of books and articles
(see also Research; Books)
benefits, 41, 78
health care and, 125, 136
business, 3347
cultural diversity, 1194
employee relations
United Kingdom, 335
human resource management, 1403, 1456, 1510, 1516, 1517, 1523
human-computer interaction, 3187
labor and work, 3426
psychology, 2896
behavioral sciences and, 3399
training and development, 3547, 3560
Accommodation
(see Disabilities)
Accounting
associations, 265
compensation arrangements, 465
Accreditation
(see also Human resource management professionals)
benefits, 73
human resource management
competency assessment, 1393, 1394
institute, 1428
self-study, 1420, 1527, 1538
senior level, 1536
organization development
concept, 2764
pension administrators, 156
Acquisitions and mergers
(see Mergers and acquisitions)
Addiction
(see Substance abuse)
Administration
(see Human resource administration; Policies)
Administrative Law Judges
administrative appeals, 1970
Adoption assistance
(see Benefits)
Advertising
recruitment, 3275, 3309, 3319, 3322
Affiliations
directory of international corporations, 3387
Affirmative action
(see also Employment law; Equal employment opportunity)
associations, 1977, 2067
cases and glossary of terms, 1973
compliance
guidelines, 1971, 2019
reference, 2023
Connecticut, 2035
developments
information and, 2022
employment opportunities, 1648
equal opportunity developments, 2079
federal contractors, 1972
minority organizations directory, 3307
newsletter, 1978
overview, 1974
plan development, 1973, 2104
supervisory guidelines and information, 2144
Age Discrimination in Employment Act
(see also Discrimination; Employment law)
analysis, 1991
reference, 1975, 2098

Aging
(see also Older workers)
health care
research and information, 128
mid-life issues, 1215
older workers
associations, 1502
issues and resources, 3467
training and, 3637
Agreements
(see Collective bargaining; Contracts)
AIDS
approaches and policies, 1261, 1263
information and practices, 1262
laws and policies
reference and developments, 1264, 1976
testing and policy, 1360
Alliances
(see Partnering and alliances)
Allowances
(see Relocation)
Alternative dispute resolution
(see Complaint and grievance procedure; Dispute resolution; Mediation)
Alternative reward systems
(see Incentive compensation)
Americans with Disabilities Act
(see also Discrimination; Employment law)
accessible environment, 3062
compliance, 1967, 1968, 1983, 1984, 1985, 2037, 2039, 2099, 2100, 2136
substance abuse, 2259
compliance audit, 2003
developments, 1969, 1969, 2008, 2009, 2141
explanation
guidelines and model program, 1981, 1990
federal and state law
cases and, 1982, 2007, 2187
guidelines, 2107, 2176, 2185, 3116
interpretations and implementation, 1989
job analysis, 1966
job descriptions, 1035
reasonable accommodation and limits, 1062
job network, 3305
overview, 2105, 2157
implementation and, 1987
reference, 1965, 1965, 1980, 1986, 1988, 2053, 2124
Applied psychology
(see Psychology)
Appraisal systems
(see Performance management/appraisal)
Arbitration
(see also Conciliation; Labor law; Labor relations)
agreement analysis, 1730
alcohol and drugs, 1266
awards, 1733
case handling, 2206
cases and awards, 2131
database, 1823
illustrative for managers, 1696
in government, 1825
in private sector, 1840
in schools, 1807
index, 1826, 1827
patterns in rulings, 1820
reference and developments, 1828
developments, 1803, 1808, 1822
discipline cases, 1809
evidence, 1814, 1815
federal employment, 2301
forms and processes, 2725
grievances and, 1819, 1821
guide, 1829
labor contracts cases, 2310
law
reference and developments, 1824, 2226
rulings and legal issues, 1830

FIGURE 7.19.   (Continued.)

INDEX